WALKING IN ZERMATT
AND SAAS-FEE

Views of the Matterhorn from the upper Zmutt valley

WALKING IN ZERMATT AND SAAS-FEE

50 ROUTES IN THE VALAIS: MATTERTAL AND SAASTAL

by Jonathan Williams and Lesley Williams

JUNIPER HOUSE, MURLEY MOSS,
OXENHOLME ROAD, KENDAL, CUMBRIA LA9 7RL
www.cicerone.co.uk

© Jonathan & Lesley Williams 2021
First edition 2021
ISBN: 978 1 78631 075 0
Reprinted 2024 (with updates)
Printed in China on responsibly sourced paper on behalf of Latitude Press Ltd
A catalogue record for this book is available from the British Library.
All photographs are by the authors unless otherwise stated.

MIX
Paper | Supporting
responsible forestry
FSC® C010256
FSC
www.fsc.org

Route mapping by Lovell Johns www.lovelljohns.com
Contains OpenStreetMap.org data © OpenStreetMap
contributors, CC-BY-SA. NASA relief data courtesy of ESRI

Updates to this Guide

While every effort is made by our authors to ensure the accuracy of guide-books as they go to print, changes can occur during the lifetime of an edition. This guidebook was researched and written before the COVID-19 pandemic. While we are not aware of any significant changes to routes or facilities at the time of printing, it is likely that the current situation will give rise to more changes than usual. Any updates that we know of for this guide will be on the Cicerone website (www.cicerone.co.uk/1075/updates), so please check before planning your trip. We also advise that you check information about transport, accommodation and shops locally.

We are always grateful for information about any discrepancies between a guidebook and the facts on the ground, sent by email to updates@cicerone.co.uk or by post to Cicerone, Juniper House, Murley Moss, Oxenholme Road, Kendal, LA9 7RL.

Register your book: To sign up to receive free updates, special offers and GPX files where available, register your book at www.cicerone.co.uk.

Our thanks to Kev Reynolds for all his encouragement with this project, the Cicerone team who have done their (absolutely normal) great job: Andrea Grimshaw, Victoria O'Dowd, Sian Jenkins and Clare Crooke. Also Rebecca Coles for her wise words on the Mischabelhütte – thanks, Becky.

Front cover: The Matterhorn seen from the ridge above the Gornergrat station

CONTENTS

Symbols used on route maps

～	route
～	alternative route
Ⓢ Ⓢ	start point/alt start point
Ⓕ Ⓕ	finish point/alt start finish
ⓈⒻ ⓈⒻ	start/finish point/alt start/finish point
>	route direction
	glacier
	woodland
	urban areas
	regional border
	international border
▬■▬	station/railway
▲	peak
⬆ ⇧	manned/unmanned refuge
ⵊ	campsite
■	building
ⵣ ■ †	church/monastery/cross
ⵍ	castle
ⵛ	pass
•	water feature
✳	viewpoint
ⵏ	picnic area
ⵍ	cable car
ⵍ	refreshment

Relief
in metres

5000 and above
4800–5000
4600–4800
4400–4600
4200–4400
4000–4200
3800–4000
3600–3800
3400–3600
3200–3400
3000–3200
2800–3000
2600–2800
2400–2600
2200–2400
2000–2200
1800–2000
1600–1800
1400–1600
1200–1400
1000–1200
800–1000
600–800
400–600
200–400
0–200

SCALE: 1:50,000

0 kilometres 0.5   1
0 miles   0.5

Contour lines are drawn at 25m intervals and highlighted at 100m intervals.

Some stage maps are 1:50,000 expanded to 1:40,000

GPX files for all routes can be downloaded free at www.cicerone.co.uk/1075/GPX.

The cirque of peaks above Saas Fee from near Plattjen – Alphubel, Täschhorn, Dom, Lenzspitze and Nadelhorn

Mountain safety

Every mountain walk has its dangers, and those described in this guidebook are no exception. All who walk or climb in the mountains should recognise this and take responsibility for themselves and their companions along the way. The author and publisher have made every effort to ensure that the information contained in this guide was correct when it went to press, but, except for any liability that cannot be excluded by law, they cannot accept responsibility for any loss, injury or inconvenience sustained by any person using this book.

International distress signal *(emergency only)*
Six blasts on a whistle (and flashes with a torch after dark) spaced evenly for one minute, followed by a minute's pause. Repeat until an answer is received. The response is three signals per minute followed by a minute's pause.

Helicopter rescue
The following signals are used to communicate with a helicopter:

Help needed: raise both arms above head to form a 'Y'

Help not needed: raise one arm above head, extend other arm downward

Emergency telephone numbers
If telephoning from the UK the dialling code is: 0041
Switzerland: OCVS (Organisation Cantonale Valaisanne de Secours): tel 144

Weather reports
Switzerland: tel 162 (in French, German or Italian), www.meteoschweiz.ch/en

Mountain rescue can be very expensive – be adequately insured.

Note on Mapping

The route maps in this guide are derived from publicly available data, databases and crowd-sourced data. As such they have not been through the detailed checking procedures that would generally be applied to a published map from an official mapping agency, although we have reviewed them closely in the light of local knowledge as part of the preparation of this guide.

ROUTE SUMMARY TABLE

Route	Walk title	Distance (km)	Ascent (m)	Descent (m)	Grade (1–4)	Time (hr/min)	Page
Zermatt							
1	The Trift gorge and Hotel du Trift	8	720	720	2	4hr	44
2	Ascent of the Mettelhorn and Platthorn from Trift	14.5	1280	2000	4	7hr 30min	49
3	Two-day expedition – Schönbielhütte via Höhbalmen	28.5	1660	1660	3	10hr	53
4	The villages of Zmutt, Zum See and Blatten	7.5	360	360	1	2hr 30min	58
5	Balcony route to Zmutt and the Kulturweg	9	460	460	2	3hr 45min	60
6	Zermatt to Sunnegga – the Findeln villages	6	670	670	1	2hr	64
7	Gletschergarten and Gorner gorge walk	6.5	180	420	1–2	2hr	66
8	Schwarzsee and Stafelalp – under the Matterhorn	16.5	1030	1030	3	5hr 30min	70
9	Schwarzsee to the Hörnlihütte	8	720	720	3–4	4hr	74
10	The Matterhorn Glacier Trail	6.5	550	200	2	2hr 30min	77
11	Gornergrat to Riffelsee, Riffelberg and Riffelalp	6.5	40	880	2	2hr 15min	81
12	Riffelalp and a woodland walk to Grüensee	7	260	260	1	2hr	85
13	The Gornergletscher and Monte Rosa Hütte	18	1000	1000	4	8hr	89
14	The mountain restaurants of Findeln	9	80	750	1–2	2hr	93
15	Blauherd to Sunnegga via Tufteren	4	70	350	1–2	1hr 30min	96
16	The Five Lakes Walk in the Findeln valley	11	500	500	2	3hr 30min	98
17	The Oberrothorn	16.5	1320	1320	3	7hr	102

Route	Walk title	Distance (km)	Ascent (m)	Descent (m)	Grade (1–4)	Time (hr/min)	Page
18	Blauherd to Pfulwe and Täschalp	13	800	1180	3–4	5hr 15min	106
19	Täsch to Täschalp and the Täschhütte	12	1260	480	2	5hr	111
20	Täschalp to Zermatt	9.5	250	830	2	3hr	114
Grächen, Randa and the lower Mattertal							
21	The Europahütte and Hängebrücke to Täschalp	13	1480	680	3	6hr	123
22	Schaliberg alp	8.5	620	620	2–3	3hr 30min	127
23	Jungen, Sparru and the Jungtal	11	760	760	3	4–5hr	131
24	A tour of the villages – Grächen and Gasenried	6.5	230	230	1	2hr 30min	135
25	Grächen leat paths – the Chilcheri and Eggeri	11.5	340	340	1–2	3hr	139
26	The Ried glacier and the Grathorn	15	780	780	2	4hr 30min	143
27	Hannigalp to Grächen via Hohtschugge and Bärgji	6.5	100	600	1–2	2hr	148
28	Grächen to Hannigalp via Stafel	5	600	100	2–3	2hr 15min	151
29	Ascent of the Wannehorn	6.5	570	570	3	3hr 30min	154
30	The Grächen to Saas-Fee Höhenweg	17	700	1010	3	6hr 45min	158
Saas-Fee and the Saastal							
31	Fee, Almagell, Grund and the Feevispa gorge	9	350	350	1	2hr 30min	169
32	Hannig from Saas-Fee	9	560	560	2	3hr 30min	174

Route	Walk title	Distance (km)	Ascent (m)	Descent (m)	Grade (1–4)	Time (hr/min)	Page
33	The ascent of Mällig – The Ibex Trail	9	420	960	3	4hr	177
34	Gletschergrotte, Spielboden and Längflue	4.5	690	40	2	2hr 15min	180
35	The Gemsweg – a tour of the Saas-Fee valley	14	830	830	2–3	4hr 30min	184
36	The Mischabelhütte	12	1600	1600	4	7–8hr	188
37	Plattjen	8	780	780	2	4hr	192
38	The Britanniahütte by the glacier route	7	950	120	4	3hr 30min	196
39	The Britanninhütte from Plattjen	5	170	100	3–4	2hr 30min	199
40	Saas-Grund to Saas-Fee – the Kapellenweg and Saumweg	4	250	250	1	1hr 30min	203
41	Saas-Grund to Saas-Fee via Bideralp	8	610	370	2	2hr 30min	206
42	Saas-Grund to Triftalp, Kreuzboden and the Weissmieshütte	8	1200	330	2	4hr	211
43	The Gspon Höhenweg	14	850	350	3	5hr	215
44	The descent of the Saastal – Mattmark to Saas-Balen	16	170	890	1–2	4hr 30min	221
45	Almagelleralp and the Almagellerhütte	15	1230	1230	3	6hr	226
46	The höhenweg from Saas-Almagell to Kreuzboden	13	900	170	3	5hr	230
47	Furggstalden and the Furggtälli	12	700	700	2	4hr	235
48	Schwarzbergalp and circuit of the Mattmark	12	590	590	3	4hr 30min	239
49	The Monte Moro Pass	15	720	720	3	5hr	243
50	The Ofental, Jazzilücke and Antronapass	18	1090	950	3–4	6hr 45min	247

Entering Zmutt village (Walk 4)

INTRODUCTION

Flower meadows high above the Saas valley

Zermatt – big, bold and brash; fast, loose and overt. One of the capitals of world mountaineering. Surrounded by many of Europe's highest mountains, with the Matterhorn rising high in the southern sky, it is an international centre attracting visitors from all over the world.

Saas-Fee – smaller, mellower, slower perhaps, discrete. Also surrounded by large mountains, it is only slightly less famous – but a world apart – from its cousin less than 10km away.

Ever since the tragic first ascent by Whymper's party in 1865, the Matterhorn has been the iconic symbol of mountains. From children's paintings to biscuit boxes, it is written into the consciousness of mountain lovers and, indeed, most people. The Mischabel wall above Saas-Fee, however, loses nothing in comparison: four vast mountains linked by a tenuous ridge, which fill the skyline from every viewpoint.

Zermatt and Saas-Fee are the twin poles of this guide; poles apart maybe, but united in the mountains that surround them and the quality of the walking opportunities. United too in the absence of cars, which are confined to large car parks outside the resorts. Numerous lifts and mountain railways will take you high into the mountains and the glaciers and to the starting points of the major climbs. The woods, tarns and mountain inns in the valleys and middle-mountain regions provide the ingredients for gentler days.

The Mattertal branches west at Stalden and is served by road as far as Täsch and by a mountain railway all the way to Zermatt. Täsch is a quiet and cosy village. St Niklaus and Randa nestle in the valley, changing little, while family-friendly Grächen occupies a shelf above.

By contrast the Saastal, or Saas valley, is narrow and constricted in its lower part, deterring big development, but it broadens to provide a home for the several Saas villages: tiny Balen, functional Grund, quiet Almagell and, of course, Fee on the lip of its huge hanging valley that resembles a vast bowl cradled on three sides by high mountains.

The valleys are home to some of Europe's largest mountains, the Matterhorn most famously, but also the Monte Rosa massif with its eight 4000m peaks, Western Europe's largest area above 4000m; the long high ridge of the Liskamm, with Castor, Pollux and the Breithorn; and after a gap the Matterhorn itself and the Dent d'Hérens. Above the western side of the Mattertal the pyramid of the Weisshorn dominates everything else, with the Dent Blanche, Zinalrothorn and Ober Gabelhorn further west still, overshadowing the Zmutt valley.

Forming the high ridge between the Saastal and the Mattertal, the Mischabel peaks – the Täschhorn, Dom, Lenzspitze and Nadelhorn – present a mountain barrier, the preserve of mountaineers. The Alphubel and Allalinhorn, directly above Saas-Fee, continue this ridge, while the Weissmies and Lagginhorn are sited on the eastern ridge above the Saastal. Others are slightly lower; the Fletschhorn just misses the 4000m mark, while the peaks to the south on the Italian border are a modest 3000–3500m.

This is also home to some of Europe's best trekking routes. The Chamonix–Zermatt Walkers' Haute Route enters the Mattertal above St Niklaus and makes its way up the valley, with higher and lower route options shared with the Tour of Monte Rosa and the Tour of the Matterhorn. In winter and spring the skiers' Haute Route descends into Zermatt and Saas-Fee from its course through the mountains to the west. The immense 600km Swiss Route 6 passes through southern Switzerland's mountains; the Alpine Passes Route explores both valleys on the *höhenwegs* (high-altitude trails) above the Saastal – Gspon and Grächen; while the Europaweg trail, often changed or re-routed due to rockfall onto the lower paths from the mountains above, makes its two-day journey from Grächen to Zermatt.

Zermatt and Saas-Fee serve as the two main bases for the walker, while Grächen provides a base for routes

in the Lower Mattertal. Walkers can choose between easier and harder routes from each village or take advantage of the many lifts. Visitors to the Saas villages benefit from concessionary passes that provide free access to the lifts and buses, while Zermatt offers a range of reductions, providing access to all levels within the valleys and making the cost of a holiday much more manageable.

THE WALKING

As high mountain villages, Zermatt and Saas-Fee have a full range of facilities of all standards, as well as transport and access to the very highest mountains and a range of superb walking in the shadows of numerous 4000m peaks. Cable cars take you up to many high points in each valley,

providing wonderful mountain views; the lift network is ready-made for the walker.

The walks range from straightforward strolls to mountain restaurants, lakes and viewpoints that may take a couple of hours with modest up and down, through to serious mountain challenges: all-day walks with glacier crossings, exposure and cable support. In-between, and comprising most of the guide, are mountain paths with short and long walks to mountain huts and cols and even a few walking 'peaks'.

Conditions underfoot vary as well. Some walks follow old tracks and mule paths (*saumwege*) or water leats (*wasserleitung*). Most walks are on well-made and maintained mountain paths with traditional red-and-white signage, while some

17

follow steep, rocky high alpine trails with handholds, metal steps and long drops. But mostly the walking is on solid paths, with the occasional excitement.

So, the walking is varied; short, straightforward routes in the valleys lead to restaurants and waterfalls. Middle-mountain walks take in high restaurants and cols, and higher routes climb to high walking peaks and huts. There is choice for everyone here.

THE VALLEYS

Life in the valleys has been determined by the ebb and flow of glaciers and the affairs of the Rhône valley and lowland Switzerland. The glaciers almost disappeared in the early Middle Ages, and both the Mattertal and Saastal became significant trade and migration routes between Switzerland and Italy. From the 17th century onwards, during the Little Ice Age, glaciers grew to their greatest extent, peaking in the middle of the 19th century as the first climbers began to scale the peaks. The settlement of these valleys is some of the earliest in the Alps; records show the establishment of churches in the 9th century. The Valais was a self-governing region before the emergence of the Swiss Confederation after the Napoleonic wars and, like all Swiss cantons, retains a strong independence.

Life in the valleys was based on farming, and evidence of this hard life can still be seen in the villages above Zermatt, Zmutt, Jungen and the Saastal. In summer sheep, goats and cattle grazed the alps, and in winter the animals lived in farm buildings beneath the family home. Some vestiges of this way of life can still be seen in the farming communities today and in the festivals that celebrate the beginning and end of summer as animals are moved to and from high pastures. Goats symbolically parade through Zermatt daily as a reminder of the roots of the region.

Linguistically the language is German, or more accurately Schweizerdeutsch, although if you speak regular German you will be readily understood. French and English are also widely understood and spoken. A valley patois remains, detectable mainly on signpost spellings, with elements of German, Italian (spoken just over the border) and French (used in the valleys until early modern times). For a list of useful German terms see Appendix C.

The tourist industry that now forms the basis of the valley economies started with the arrival of mountaineers, who came first to admire and then to scale the peaks. The earliest ascents in the valleys were of the Weissmies in 1855 by Peter Joseph Zurbriggen and Jakob Christian Häuser, and of the various peaks of the Monte Rosa by Rev Charles Hudson and others in the same year. The first ascent of the Matterhorn in 1865 marked the end of this 'golden age' of mountaineering, when first

Traditional alpenhorns at Riffelalp

ascents were made of all major mountains in the Alps and mountaineering developed in new directions.

THE MATTERHORN

The Matterhorn was one of the last 4000m mountains to be climbed in 1865, resulting in one of climbing's first and most famous (or notorious) accidents. Edward Whymper set out to reach the summit before his erstwhile partner and guide, Jean-Antoine Carrel from Valtournenche, who was on the Italian side of the mountain. Whymper's party included Chamonix guide Michel Croz and Zermatt guides Peter Taugwalder and his son (also Peter), Lord Francis Douglas, the Rev Charles Hudson and Douglas Hadow, an inexperienced English aristocrat. It was a first attempt on the Hörnli ridge from Zermatt, previous attempts being on the Italian ridge. On the descent from the summit, Hadow slipped and Douglas, Hudson, Croz and Hadow fell to their deaths; Whymper and the Taugwalders survived. Carrel's party was some 200m below the summit when Whymper summitted. (Apparently Whymper rolled rocks down the Italian face to grab Carrel's attention and 'inform' him of his success!) Carrel retreated and led the second ascent three days later. The first woman to reach the summit was Englishwoman Lucy Walker alongside guide Melchior Anderegg in 1871, again in rivalry with another climber, the American Meta Brevoort.

The descent to Stafelalp passes under the north face of the Matterhorn (Walk 8)

THE SHAPE OF THE MOUNTAINS

The Alps are relatively young mountains in geological time, having formed between 40 and 25 million years ago when the African plate and Eurasian plates collided, pressing and folding the continental crust and forcing both plates upwards while the bulk of the African plate slid over the top. This caused the Eurasian plate to become squashed and stretched beneath it. What this all means in terms of the mountains in the area is interesting. Much of the bulk of the Matterhorn, Dent Blanche, Ober Gabelhorn, Zinalrothorn and Weisshorn is made up of Gneiss from the ancient African continental plate. The rock is a very different colour and sits on top of younger rocks that originated in ancient oceans. The huge Rhône valley to the north of the Mattertal and Saastal was caused by a fault line, and the glaciers and river that carved their way through simply followed a natural line of weakness.

Glaciers have shaped the mountains and valleys we see today. The main valleys were carved by huge glaciers during several ice ages, creating their distinctive U shape, while the narrow gorges in the lower sections of both the Mattertal and Saastal were carved by water finding ways through the rocks, exploiting fractures and areas of weakness. The hanging valley in which Saas-Fee sits was formed as the relative power of the glacier in the main valley continued to erode the rock more deeply, and for longer, leaving the tributary valley higher above. In the museum in Saas-Fee you will find early photographs

The Grenzgletscher stretches down from the Monte Rosa (left) and Liskamm (right) (Walk 11)

showing the glaciers stretching down almost to Saas-Fee. In the mid 19th century one unfortunate village was destroyed by an advancing glacier. How things have changed in recent times; the bare, scoured rock immediately below the snouts of all the glaciers bears testament to the rapid retreat of the ice.

PLANTS AND WILDLIFE

For much of the year the alpine slopes in both the Mattertal and Saastal are covered with snow. The blanket of snow acts as protection for hardy little plants, providing shelter from harsh winds, insulation from the bitter cold, and moisture while the plants rest in a semi-hibernating state. All this changes as soon as the snow begins to melt, with myriad varieties of alpine flowers blooming in succession in the short summer season. The first to appear is the alpine snowbell (*Soldanella*), tiny fringed pink/purple flowers supported on thin stems. In June more plants come into flower, mainly pink or purple in colour, including the carthusian pink (a relative of the garden pink), cowberry and varieties of campion, stonecrop, saxifrage, orchid and cinquefoil. In July the alpenrose transforms many of the hillsides in the area into a sea of vivid rose red. This slow-growing plant takes its time but can colonise huge areas of both open hillside and lightly shaded woodland. Other flowers to look out for are the intensely blue gentian and as autumn approaches, the delicate meadow saffron or autumn crocus. To identify these, and many others you will come across,

From top: cobweb houseleek (Sempervivum arachnoideum); spring gentian (Gentiana verna); alpenrose (Rhododendron ferrugineum)

help is at hand! With photographs of flowers arranged by colour, *Alpine Flowers* by Gillian Price, published by Cicerone, provides an easy way to identify 230 alpine flowers.

Take a walk across a high alpine meadow and you may hear a piercing whistle repeated over and over again. Locate where the sound is coming from, and you should see a small brown rodent, about the size of a mountain hare, standing upright sounding the alarm. These shy creatures are marmots; they graze on vegetation in the high alps and live in burrows underground where they hibernate during the winter months. Other more noticeable inhabitants of the higher wooded slopes and rocky hillsides are chamois, with short, slender horns, which tend to live and feed in small family groups, and ibex that have longer, thicker horns. Meanwhile on the lower slopes and in woodland tiny red-black squirrels scuttle around at great speed, foraging for berries and vegetation.

The skies are the preserve of the Alpine chough, a close relative of the crow, and eagles can often be spotted riding the thermals high above the hillsides.

LONG-DISTANCE ROUTES IN THE AREA

Several trekking routes pass through the Saas valley, sections of which form parts of the walks in this guide.

Chamonix–Zermatt Walkers' Haute Route

Winding across passes between Chamonix and Zermatt, the walkers' Haute Route takes nearly two weeks to complete, crossing the Valais Canton in the southern part of Switzerland. It enters the Mattertal at the Augstbordpass above St Niklaus and descends to Jungen before making its way up the valley to Zermatt, either along the valley floor or by climbing the eastern side of the valley on the Europaweg (now partially closed) or a combination of the two.

Tour of Monte Rosa (TMR)

This renowned route runs through the Mattertal and Saastal, taking in the Grächen–Saas-Fee Höhenweg, a challenging route in its own right, described in Walk 30. It continues south and takes the Monte Moro Pass into Italy, before descending to Macugnaga and continuing south of Monte Rosa to return to Zermatt. The TMR, which can be walked in either direction, forms the basis of the Ultra Trail Monte Rosa race each September.

Alpine Passes Route (Swiss National Route 6)
This ultra-long distance trail runs from Chur in eastern Switzerland to the shores of Lac Léman. It enters the Saastal at Gspon and traverses the steep hillsides facing the Balfrin before descending to Saas-Grund and climbing back up to Saas-Fee. The route then follows the Saas-Fee–Grächen Höhenweg towards the Mattertal and the western Valais. The Gspon Höhenweg, described in Walk 43, covers most of this route, finishing at a higher point.

Tour of the Fletschhorn
This tour follows a route around the eastern mountain wall above the Saastal, including the 4000m Lagginhorn and Weissmies and the slightly lower Fletschhorn. It enters the Almagellertal by the Zwischbergen Pass and takes the high route across the eastern mountain wall to Gspon.

WHEN TO GO

The main walking season runs from mid June until mid September. Outside this period, huts may well not be open and much of the other accommodation may also be closed. However, September and October can be more settled months, and with good daytime temperatures, cooling progressively at night, and with autumn colour emerging, these are attractive months to visit, although accommodation and restaurants will close over the period.

GETTING THERE

Switzerland is very accessible and has an excellent public transport infrastructure. Zermatt and Saas-Fee are, however, some distance from the main airports or access points into the country, so it is likely that it will take at least two to three hours to reach either resort after first entering Switzerland.

By train
From the UK the trip by rail will cost a little more and take a little longer than flying, but it is perfectly feasible as well as more environmentally friendly. Take Eurostar from London St Pancras to Paris Gare du Nord, two stops in Paris on the RER (green line D) to the Gare du Lyon then TGV from Paris to Geneva or Visp. (Other routes avoiding Paris are available.) London to Visp can be booked on a single ticket through French railways (SNCF). It may be worth splitting the booking at Geneva to take advantage of discount deals and cards on both the French and Swiss railways.

Rail journeys from Belgium and the Netherlands and other points in northern Europe are also options and often shorter.

By road

Road access is through the French motorway system to Geneva or Basel or further east through Germany. You will need a Swiss motorway vignette (sticker), which currently costs CHF40 and is available online or at the border. If coming via Basel, the most direct route is via the Lötschberg Tunnel, a long railway tunnel under the Bernese Oberland from Kandersteg through which accompanied vehicles can be transported on trains. From Geneva, the motorway route is Lausanne–Martigny–Visp, Visp being the access point to the valleys. At Stalden the valleys split: the Saastal to the east, the Mattertal to the west. Copious parking is available at Täsch (CHF14.50 per day) and Saas-Fee (CHF13 per day, CHF77 per week with the Citizens' Pass – see 'Discount cards'). Lower in the valleys there are smaller public car parks as well as parking at some accommodation.

By air

Switzerland's main airports are Geneva and Zurich. From each of these it is possible to book trains right through to Zermatt (3hr 50min from Geneva airport and 3hr 30min from Zurich). For the Saas villages, leave the train at Visp or Stalden and continue by bus. Geneva and Zurich are served by both low-cost and full-service airlines within Europe, from the UK and internationally. For flight information visit www.skyscanner.net and www.kayak.co.uk.

Discount cards

The SNCF offers a broad range of discount cards, including a senior card for the over 60s.

In Switzerland, the main card to consider is the Half-Price Card, currently CHF120 for one month. This provides half-price travel throughout the country, including buses, trains and cable cars, so it is a good deal. The saving on the return journey from Geneva or Zurich to Zermatt or Saas-Fee almost covers the cost of the card, so all additional travel thereafter benefits. An alternative option is the Swiss Pass, available for shorter periods, providing unlimited use of bus, train and lake ferry routes.

The Swiss travel passes, of which there are many options, are referred to above.

Travel within the Mattertal is almost entirely by train. The Saastal has no trains, and buses make up the public transport system. In each case regular services operate at least hourly, and often more frequently, between the various villages and walking locations. Buses are post-buses, providing a comprehensive transport service in the valleys, running from early morning to late evening. Services are punctual and reliable, and delays are rare.

In Zermatt a range of day passes and a longer Peak Pass cover transport costs, but the Half-Price Card is

often the better option. In the Saastal a passport or Citizens' Pass, issued free by all accommodation providers, gives free access to lifts and buses in and around the villages. Grächen's Gold Card provides local benefits (see Grächen section).

Lifts

Cable cars, mountain railways, funiculars, gondolas and chairlifts are an integral part of the Alpine walking experience. The Saas valley's lifts are covered by the Citizens' Pass, while Zermatt offers a range of passes, including the Half-Price Card. The lifts are expensive if you turn up for a day trip without a pass. Only a mountain aesthete, or a guidebook writer, would eschew the chance to be lifted 1000m

up the mountain in 15mins and start from there. The main lifts and their current opening periods and running times are given in the introduction to each valley.

ACCOMMODATION

A wide range of good accommodation is available throughout the valleys. There are outstanding tourist offices in each village, as well as helpful websites (see Appendix A), to help the visitor make the most of their trip.

Camping

There are four campsites in the Saastal and three in the Mattertal (see Appendix A). Prices vary but are generally between CHF9 and CHF14 plus a tourist tax of CHF3 per person per night, and between CHF6 and CHF10 for tents. With plentiful local restaurants as well as supermarkets, this is a good, low-cost option.

Apartments
As these centres are also busy winter resorts, there are many apartments available to rent in the summer. Prices outside Zermatt may be around CHF600 per week for very good 2-bedroom, 4-person apartments. Zermatt is more expensive at CHF1000 or more per week.

Hotels
There is a wide range of hotels, from the simple to the height of luxury, details of which are available through the tourist offices or directly online.

Huts and berghotels (mountain inns)
It is quite possible to use mountain huts and other mountain accommodation as a base for a few days. Mountain huts (*hütte*) are either operated by the Swiss Alpine Club (SAC) or are privately owned. A *berghotel* (or *berggasthaus*) is privately run, often offering more private accommodation, but still providing communal sleeping in dormitories (*lager*). Overnight stays will usually cost in the range of CHF50–70 per person, including dinner and breakfast. All will provide a picnic lunch, if requested in good time, at an additional cost.

OTHER LOCAL FACILITIES
All the larger villages have a range of shops and restaurants, and most have at least one bank with a cashpoint. There are outdoor stores in Zermatt, Saas-Fee and Grächen, as well as other sports shops and wellness services.

The main hospital is in Visp. Zermatt, Saas-Fee, Saas-Grund and Grächen all have pharmacies and doctors, as do St Niklaus and Stalden.

MOUNTAIN HUTS

Visiting one or more mountain huts and, better still, spending a couple of nights up high, is a quintessential part of the Swiss mountain walking experience. For many it's a new experience, but it is easy to get the hang of it.

On arrival change into hut shoes, either the ones provided (usually crocs or similar) or ones you have brought yourself. Check in with the guardian or guardienne who manages the hut: he/she will allocate a bed/space in the dorm for you and your party. Blankets or duvets and pillows are provided in the dormitories, but you will need a sleeping bag liner – these can be rented in most huts, so check when you call to book; silk ones are lighter and more comfortable.

Do book ahead – huts may be busy and staff need to plan meals in advance. Most hut staff speak some English, but it's a good opportunity to unleash your inner linguist. If your plans change, or if you are unable to get to the hut, call to let them know. Failing to arrive at a scheduled hut may lead to a search being instigated if you are thought to have gone missing.

Meals are taken communally and the guardian will allocate seating. Dinner is generally at 1800 or 1900 but check on arrival. Meals vary but will often start with soup, followed by salad, main course and a simple dessert. You will be asked about your breakfast time – for walkers normally between 0600 and 0700. Settle your bill either after dinner or in the morning. Before you depart, leave your bed space tidy, folding all blankets and other bedding, and check you have got all your kit.

Sleeping is usually either in 4–8 person rooms or in a larger dorm. Bedtime is generally before 2200, when the hut goes quiet and the late-night rustling of plastic bags is to be avoided. Huts also serve climbers, who may slip out any time after 0200 depending on their route. Sort your bed out early, keep your gear tucked away and tidy, get washing and personal tasks out of the way and then settle back to enjoy the late afternoon and evening. Take in the views, the sunsets and sunrises and enjoy the chance to make new friends, new memories and new plans.

WEATHER

In southern Switzerland, close to the Italian border, the valleys have a good climate. Saas-Fee claims to enjoy 300 days per year of sunshine. However, high in the mountains, local factors may have a greater impact on the weather. Hot air rising from Italy and the Swiss valleys can bring storms, and the normal Alpine thunderstorms of late afternoon will occur throughout the summer, particularly on humid days. Heatwaves affecting the rest of Europe also affect the valleys, but the altitude and the dryness of the mountain air make them more manageable. In June and well into July, there may be late-lying snow above 2000m. Check conditions before arriving – there are many webcams, so it is possible to inspect the mountainsides directly. Tourist offices will have a clear if perhaps cautious view on which routes are open.

In the summer, late-lying snow will be soft and frustrating. In more exposed places, however, often on north-facing slopes and other sheltered places where there is less direct sunshine, it is possible to come

ZERMATT TEMPERATURE AND RAINFALL						
	May	June	July	August	September	October
Average high (°C)	20	23	25	24	20	14
Average low (°C)	7	10	11	11	7	2
Average daily hours of sunshine	6.6	7.7	8.6	7.5	6.3	5.1
Average monthly rainfall (mm)	39	47	49	63	45	46

Source: weatherandclimate.com Sion weather station data

across hard snow (*névé*) or even ice, so look out for this and unless you are equipped with axe, crampons and poles take another route.

Temperature and rainfall statistics for Zermatt over the summer months are shown in the table.

MAPS

Swiss mapping is excellent and clear. However, it is crucial you buy a Wanderkarte, a map marked with the footpath network – versions without the paths highlighted may be things of beauty, but they are very difficult to use for walking.

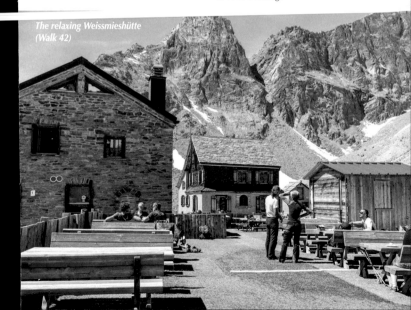

The relaxing Weissmieshütte (Walk 42)

Recommended maps are as follows:

- **Swisstopo 3306T Zermatt–Saas-Fee at 1:33,000 1km = 3cm** is essentially a blown-up 1:50,000 scale covering the Zermatt and Saas-Fee centres, including the surrounding mountains but only extending as far north as Täsch and Saas-Balen. Water resistant.
- **Swisstopo 5028T Monte Rosa – Matterhorn at 1:50,000, 1km = 2cm** comprises high-quality mapping in the Swiss style but the scale is perhaps a bit big for walking.
- **Kümmerly + Frey Zermatt and Saas-Fee at 1:60,000, 1km = 2.5cm** covers the whole valley, including Grächen; a match for the Swisstopo in clarity. Water resistant.
- **Rotten Verlag publishes three maps at a scale of 1:25,000**, one each for Zermatt, Grächen/ St Niklaus and Saas-Fee. These maps show path numbers, walking times and outline a few walking routes. Although showing more paths at a small scale on a similar base, these can feel a bit harder to use than some of the others.

Map sources are given in Appendix A.

The route maps provided in this guidebook are at 1:50,000, 2cm = 1km. These are derived from open-source data but have been reviewed in detail by the authors. Spellings and heights have been standardised as far as possible against Swisstopo mapping, but be aware that different maps have a range of heights and that signpost heights and spellings may differ from those on the maps.

APPS

In our digital world, apps are a valable component of the walker's toolkit. The valley is covered by many digital mapping resources, such as ViewRanger and PhoneMaps. The following apps are specifically recommended for the walking visitor.

Mapping – Swisstopo provides access to all the Swiss mapping databases, in online and offline (downloadable) formats. Different tiles can be selected and bought, but it is crucial to download the footpath layer.

Travel – SBB is a complete Swiss travel app for trains, buses and connecting cable cars, as well as some other services. The app brings together the entirety of the Swiss public transport system into a seamless whole. It's easy to use, linking with online payments and storing your Half-Price Card as well, thereby automatically accessing half-price fares. Note that if you do have a Half-Price Card, you will need to show a printout when tickets are inspected.

Weather – MeteoSchweiz/ MeteoSuisse is a weather app from the Swiss meteorological agency that has full forecasting capabilities. It takes a little time to get the hang of, as it has lots of resources to explore, but it's worth the effort and is a bit more accurate than more general weather apps that don't fully account for Swiss mountain conditions.

Resort Information – Matterhorn and Saas-Fee apps are free to download and contain detailed information about the facilities in each location.

EQUIPMENT

You shouldn't need an ice axe and crampons on most of these routes, certainly after mid July. However, crampons are needed for the Monte Rosa Hütte and the Mettelhorn routes, and also early in the summer when there is snow lying on the ground.

If you plan to tackle harder routes in early summer, an ice axe and crampons could be a useful addition

assuming you have the space to carry them and the necessary mountaineering experience to use them. If you decide to hire a guide to do a climb, you can also hire the required gear.

Likewise, via ferrata protection (harness, lanyard, helmet) is not required unless you want to tackle some of the local via ferratas (see Zermatt and Saas-Fee introductions).

PREPARATION

It is much better to be fit before starting a Swiss mountain walking holiday. If you are hill fit for your home country, you will have few or no issues. Even a few lower walks will help with your preparation, especially if you manage two or three days together in walking boots and carrying a rucksack it also help in i

Jungen and the view up towards the Jungtal (Walk 23)

your acclimatisation to the higher altitude. At 1600m and 1800m you may feel little effect, but over 2500m the effect of the altitude will kick in, and you should gain height progressively before going far above 3000m. If you develop a headache, the best thing to do is to descend.

USING THIS GUIDE

This guide provides 50 walking routes split between Zermatt and the upper Mattertal, Grächen, Randa and the lower Mattertal and Saas-Fee, the main centre of the Saastal. Each section starts with an introduction on the valley base and its surrounding villages, followed by detailed route descriptions of the walks from each centre.

Distance, walking time, ascent and descent for each route are shown, together with a broad grade or indication of difficulty. Access is outlined and the main refreshment opportunities are mentioned.

Walking times
The walking times in this guide will usually agree with the signposted times on the yellow signs throughout the valleys. They are based on the steady pace of a reasonably fit hill/mountain walker and don't allow for stops, lunch, afternoon cake, long siestas or photo sessions, so in practice you will need to adjust these timings to match your own preferences. A five-hour walking day with several long stops might result in seven to eight hours on the mountain.

On the approach to Grüensee with views back to the Zinalrothorn and Ober Gabelhorn (Walk 12)

You should also consider your fitness and acclimatisation. Even if you are fit, take time to get used to the altitude. If you are flying in from abroad, bear in mind that the combined effect of jet lag and altitude can be challenging, throwing all walking times into disarray, so do make allowances in the first few days of a trip and start with some easier routes. In most cases, times that were challenging at the start of a holiday will seem much easier by the end of a week or two.

Grades

Swiss paths are graded into three levels of path:

Hiking trails (*wanderwege, chemins pédestres*) don't place any particular demands on the walker. They are marked on the ground in yellow or with yellow diamonds (not to

be confused with the signposts, which are also yellow).

Mountain hiking trails (*bergwanderwege, chemins de randonnée de montagne*) require walkers to be sure-footed, unafraid of heights, physically fit and experienced in the mountains. They are signposted with red-and-white waymarks or pointers on the yellow signposts.

Alpine trails (*alpine wanderwege, chemins de randonnée alpine*) demand that users are sure-footed, unafraid of heights and physically very fit; alpine experience and additional mountain equipment may be required. The paths are marked with blue-and-white waymarks or blue signs.

Most paths are well graded. Yellow paths are easy; blue paths are hard. Red-and-white paths, the mountain hiking trails, cover a wide range of

Gradings used in this guide	
Grade 1	An easy walk, mainly on undemanding, yellow paths or tracks, but likely with some red-and-white sections, in the valley or just above.
Grade 2	A moderate walk on clear and mainly straightforward mountain paths. No significant exposure or problematic ground on the route; however, the route may still be long, with considerable up and down and an occasional rail or steps.
Grade 3	A harder mountain walk on higher red-and-white mountain paths. Ascents, descents and walk times will be long, and in places there may be trickier ground, exposure and aided sections (cables, steps, ladders). Situated further away from valley bases and habitation.
Grade 4	A high, hard mountain walk, usually taking in parts of the blue alpine trail. Considerable ascent and descent will be involved, the ground will be rough and rocky, there may be exposed passages and there will probably be aided sections with cables, steps and ladders. These may include straightforward glacier crossings.

Signpost indicating alpine (blue/white), mountain (red/white) and easy hiking paths (yellow)

walking, so we have provided a more nuanced grading structure (see table).

Bear in mind that a route is given a grade as a whole, so there may be an occasional harder section on a Grade 2 route, and a Grade 4 may have substantial sections of easier walking.

It's important to note that as snow and ice on mountain slopes melt, landslides can occur and paths can become damaged by subsidence from below or stonefall from above, so take account of the path conditions as you find them and alter your plans accordingly.

Equipment
For all except a few routes in this book, no special equipment beyond regular hiking gear is needed.

Good footwear comes first. Boots are recommended: light to mid-weight is ideal, but many walkers are happy using trainers or approach shoes. Use what you would generally use on a rocky hike.

Good waterproofs are next. You may see no rain whatsoever for the whole of a two-week holiday, but mountain weather is changeable, so you may experience rain daily. Late afternoon thunderstorms are likely to be the main issue, so the best plan is to finish the day in good time; a thunderstorm can make you wet and cold very quickly. And if a low-pressure zone settles over southern Switzerland, it could be dreary for a day or two. A modern, light to mid-weight jacket and waterproof trousers are quite adequate for these routes.

You will also need a suitable rucksack to carry your waterproofs, food for the day, spare fleece, hat, gloves, first-aid kit, water, camera, etc. A 20–30 litre rucksack is ample.

GPX TRACKS
GPX tracks for the routes in this guidebook are available to download free at www.cicerone.co.uk/1075/GPX. A GPS device is an excellent aid to navigation, but you should also carry a map and compass and know how to use them. GPX files are provided in good faith, but neither the author nor the publisher accepts responsibility for their accuracy.

ZERMATT AND
THE MATTERTAL

Looking across to the Matterhorn from the high path to Zmutt (Walk 5)

Zermatt overview

SWITZERLAND

Weiss

Zinalrothorn

Ober
Gabelhorn

Rothornhü

Dent
Blanche

Hotel du

Ferpècle Glacier

Schönbielhütte

Zmutt

Hotel Silvana

Zmuttgletscher

Schwarzsee **8**

9

Hörnlihütte

10

Dent d'Hérens

Matterhorn

ITALY

N

Breuil-
Cervinia

0   2   4 km

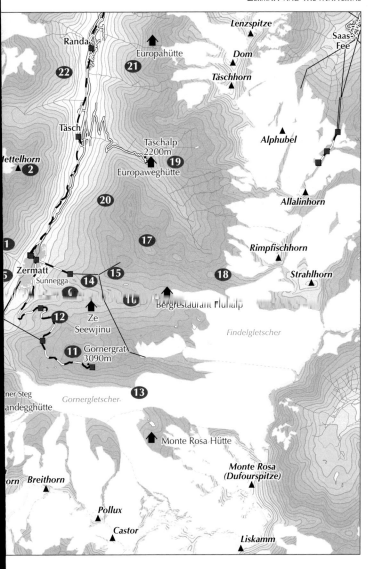

Randa

22

Europahütte

21

Lenzspitze

Saas Fee

Dom

Täschhorn

Täsch

Täschalp
2200m

19

Europaweghütte

Mettelhorn

2

Alphubel

20

17

Allalinhorn

1

Zermatt

Sunnegga

5

14

15

18

Rimpfischhorn

Strahlhorn

16

Bergrestaurant Fluhalp

12

Ze
Seewjinu

11

Gornergrat
3090m

Findelgletscher

ner Steg

andegghütte

Gornergletscher

13

Monte Rosa Hütte

Monte Rosa
(Dufourspitze)

orn

Breithorn

Pollux

Castor

Liskamm

Hiking trails provide superb views of Monte Rosa, Liskamm, Castor, Pollox, the Breithorn and the Matterhorn

At Stalden the Vispertal valley forks; to the east lies the Saastal and its river, the Sasservispa, while to the west, and running straight ahead, is the Mattertal and its river, the Mattervispa. Between Stalden and St Niklaus the Mattertal runs through a deep and narrow gorge that opens out at St Niklaus. Perched on a sunny ledge above St Niklaus is the small resort of Grächen (covered in Part 2, Grächen is a base for routes in the lower Mattertal). Ahead the valley passes Herbriggen, Randa and Täsch, where cars must be left, before climbing to the world-famous, car-free Alpine town of Zermatt.

The valley is lined on both sides by ranks of 4000m peaks. To the east lie the Mischabel peaks – the Dom (4546m), Nadelhorn (4327m), Lenzspitze (4294m) and Täschhorn (4491m), with shyer peaks hiding behind. To the west are the Weisshorn (4506m), Zinalrothorn (4221m) and Ober Gabelhorn (4063m), again with more major mountains behind. The steepness of the mountainsides means there are only a few walkers' routes in the high mountains along the length of the valley (see Part 2, Walks 21 to 23).

Täsch has a modern underground car park, leaving unspoilt green meadows surrounding the peaceful village. Above Täsch the cog railway grinds out the final kilometres into Zermatt. Zermatt Bahnhofstrasse, the main street, is at the northern end of town and you can get around the sprawling resort either on foot or by one of the electric buses or taxis that buzz in a carefree manner through the narrow streets. As well as being a bustling town, Zermatt is a stop-off on Europe's must-see tick list, so it accommodates visitors young and old, and of all nationalities, who are attracted by the shops and restaurants as much as the magnificent peaks above.

Three great valleys lead out of the town; to the east the Findeln valley heads for several kilometres into quiet walking terrain interspersed with attractive lakes and mountain restaurants. At its head lie the Rimpfischhorn and Strahlhorn, then the Findelngletscher, which only 50 years ago came down as far as Grüensee lake, followed by the start of the Monte Rosa range, the aptly named Nordend.

To the south, the bulk of the rocky ridge of the Gornergrat obscures the Gornergletscher behind and the surrounding peaks: the 4000m summits of Monte Rosa (4634m), the Liskamm (4527m), the 'twins' Castor (4223m) and Pollux (4092m) and the bulky Breithorn (4159m).

The Zmutt valley, running beneath the Matterhorn, lies to the west, extending for 12km before glaciers take over at the foot of the 4478m Matterhorn, which commands attention at every turn. Its legendary north face, often snow-covered even in summer, looms over the valley. Behind it the shapely Dent d'Hérens is hidden from all who fail to venture to the end of the valley, while the Dent Blanche and Ober Gabelhorn and their outliers face the Matterhorn.

VALLEY BASES

Randa is a low-key village that can be accessed by rail and road. It has a hotel and several apartments for rent. It is a good starting point for routes up to the Europahütte and above, as well as walks on the slopes below the Weisshorn. The tourist office is next to the station.

Täsch is a quiet and attractive village with several routes rising to Täschalp and the Täschhütte. Facilities include several shops and a supermarket, a tourist office opposite the station, hotels, restaurants and a campsite. For those looking for the attractions of Zermatt at a lower cost, it is possible to stay in Täsch and take the train into town for excursions, although at some point the travel time (30–45min) and related costs will balance out the savings.

Traffic-free **Zermatt** is one of the world's great mountain resorts. The Matterhorn looms high above the town, and the myths and tragedies surrounding this iconic peak are central to Zermatt's appeal. There are plenty of hotels, apartments and other types of accommodation, so a bed can usually be found – although at a price. Shops of all shapes and sizes line the main street. The supermarkets and outdoor stores are concentrated near the station, and there are bakeries dotted around throughout the town. The tourist office is located just outside the station. All travel around Zermatt is by foot, bike or electric taxi. It takes around 15–20 minutes to walk from the station to the main lift station, the Matterhorn Glacier Paradise cable car, at the southern end of the town, which rises to Furi, Trockener Steg, Klein Matterhorn and the Matterhorn Alpine Crossing.

Hotels are concentrated around the Bahnhofstrasse and near the church, spilling across the river. Further out, chalets and apartments are the norm. The quieter 'suburb' of Winkelmatten, 15 minutes from the centre, is served by a bakery; this area will suit visitors looking for a more peaceful stay. For those who want to be closer to the action, it's better to stay nearer the town centre.

LIFTS AND MOUNTAIN RAILWAYS

The **Sunnegga underground** funicular starts close to the centre of town,

on the right-hand bank of the river. It provides access to the mountainside immediately above Zermatt, with onward lifts to the Blauherd station and the Unterrothorn at 3104m. In July and August it operates from 0800 to 1800 to and from Sunnegga, and from 0810 to 1700 to and from Blauherd. Prices are from CHF26.50 Sunnegga return and CHF60 Blauherd return. The Rothorn lift was being refurbished in 2019 but is expected to reopen in the future.

The **Gornergrat mountain railway** starts opposite Zermatt's main station and winds its way to the summit of the Gornergrat, stopping at Riffelalp, Riffelberg and Rotenboden. It is the best way to access the walking options on the bulky 3000m Gornergrat mountain area. In July and August it runs from 0700 to 1800. The

Zermatt's bustling main street

The Gornergrat railway provides easy access to walks and views of the Matterhorn (Walk 12)

adult price to Gornergrat is CHF119 return. Afternoon and one-way tickets are considerably lower.

The **Matterhorn Glacier Paradise** lift system starts at the *talstation* (bottom station) at the southern end of Zermatt. Steady streams of walkers and sightseers make their way there each morning. An initial climb to the interchange at the hamlet of Furi accesses lifts onto the Riffelberg and ahead to Schwarzsee and Trockener Steg (2939m) and the Klein Matterhorn (at 3883m the highest cable car in Europe). In July and August lifts run to and from Furi from 0630 to 1750, with the final return from Matterhorn Glacier Paradise at 1630. Prices are from over CHF20 Furi return, and CHF120 Glacier Paradise return. A combined Gornergrat/Glacier Paradise ticket is also available.

Recent construction of a cableway between the Klein Matterhorn (3883m) and Testa Grigia (3479m) on the Italian frontier means that it is possible to visit Cervinia on the Italian side of the Matterhorn entirely by cable car, but at a price! A return trip from Zermatt is around CHF200.

MOUNTAIN HUTS, BERGHOTELS AND RESTAURANTS

Zermatt is surrounded by a network of mountain huts, *berghotels* and restaurants. These make good destinations for a day's walk or an overnight stay. There are also several sizeable hotels on the Gornergrat. The main places of interest to walkers – establishments providing meals and walkers' accommodation – are listed below and are shown on the Zermatt overview map. (For tips on staying in a mountain hut, see the Introduction.)

Hotel du Trift (2337m) This privately run *berghotel*, which sits at the head of the Trift gorge, was built in 1900 and has changed little since. Just over a 2hr walk above Zermatt, it is situated on Walks 1–3 to the Mettelhorn and Schönbielhütte. It has space for 19 in rooms and 30 in dormitory accommodation and is open end of June to mid September. Tel +41 79 408 70 20, www.zermatt.net/trift.

Rothornhütte (3198m) This accommodation is the starting point for mountaineers climbing the Zinalrothorn, Wellenkuppe, Ober Gabelhorn and Trifthorn. It has 68 beds and is open mid July to mid September. Tel +41 79 132 12 05, rothornhuette.sac@gmail.com.

Schönbielhütte (2694m) This mountain hut is the start/finish point for the Chamonix–Zermatt glacier/ski touring Haute Route. It has 80 beds and is open end of March to mid September. Tel +41 27 967 13 54, bielti.zermatt@gmx.ch.

Hörnlihütte (3260m) Principally for climbers tackling the Matterhorn, this mountain hut is very expensive. It has 130 beds in rooms of 3–8 beds and is open July to September. Tel +41 27 967 22 64, www.hoern lihuette.ch.

Gandegghütte (3030m) Situated above Trockener Stegg, close to glaciers, this traditional mountain hut has 50 beds in rooms and dormitories and is open mid June to mid September. Tel +41 79 607 88 68, www.gandegg.ch

Hotel Silvana (Furi) (1900m) Located a few yards from the Matterhorn Express cable car, this mountain hotel has 40 beds in rooms and is open end of June to end of September. Tel +41 27 966 28 00, www.hotelsilvana.ch.

Monte Rosa Hütte (2883m) This mountain hut, situated at the foot of the Monte Rosa massif, has 120 beds and is open July to mid September. Tel +41 27 967 21 15, www.monterosa huette.ch.

Ze Seewjinu (2300m) (Ze Seewjinen on the Swisstopo map) Situated between Gornergrat and Rothorn, this mountain lodge has both rooms and dormitory accommodation. It is open July to mid October. Tel +41 79 900 23 00, www.zeseewjinu.ch.

Bergrestaurant Fluhalp (2620m) At the head of the Findeln valley, this mountain inn has 45 beds in rooms and a dormitory and is open end of June to end of September. Tel +41 27 967 25 97, www.fluhalp-zermatt.ch.

Täschhütte (2701m) High above the Täsch valley and offering 80 beds in dormitories, this mountain hut is open end of June to end of September. Tel +41 27 967 39 13, www.taeschhuette.ch.

Täschalp Lodge and Restaurant (2225m) Situated in Täschalp, this family-run mountain hut has 30 beds and is open mid June to end of

September. Tel +41 27 967 23 01, www.taschalp.ch/lodge.

Larger hotels can be found at Schwarzsee, Gornergrat, Riffelberg and Riffelalp.

All mountain huts serve meals. Additionally, mountain restaurants are spread throughout the valley and make good refreshment stops or destinations in themselves if food with a view is the purpose of your day's walk. The main locations are (broadly anti-clockwise around Zermatt) Alterhaupt (Edelweiss), Stafelalp, Zmutt, Zum See, Blatten, a concentration around the Furi cable car station, Riffelberg, Riffelalp, Findeln, Sunnegga, Tufteren and Ried. Cable car stations also generally have restaurants and other facilities.

ZERMATT PASSES

The cable cars and the Gornergrat train are expensive. Unlike in Saas-Fee where a free pass is provided for visitors staying there, there is no such system giving free access to all transport in Zermatt. If you've bought the Half-Price card, it will work on trains and lifts. Failing that, a range of daily and weekly Peak Passes are available (from about CHF150/day to CHF250/week), offering senior, child and group discounts; bikes are also covered. More information can be found at www.zermatt.ch or at the Gornergratbahn or cable car stations.

OTHER ACTIVITIES

A huge range of other mountain activities are possible in Zermatt, including climbing, mountaineering, glacier skiing at the Klein Matterhorn and via ferratas. Mountain biking is especially popular, but scooters, electric bikes, mountain carting, culinary trips, golf, fly fishing, a summer open-air theatre on the Gornergrat and children's play groups are also all available. On wet days the Zermatt museum is worth a visit, but the weather changes quickly so even on a wet day, by watching the weather and checking the forecast, some outdoor activity is generally possible.

The Gornergrat train approaching its summit station

WALK 1
The Trift gorge and Hotel du Trift

Start/finish	Zermatt, 1620m
Distance	8km
Total ascent/descent	720m
Grade	2
Time	4hr
Max altitude	Trift, 2337m
Refreshments	Edelweiss restaurant and hotel at Alterhaupt, Hotel du Trift

The ascent of the Trift gorge with its two mountain restaurants is one of the classic walks from Zermatt, and it is accessible directly from the centre of the town. The gorge carries the Triftbach stream down in a series of cascades from its origins in the Triftgletscher high above, while the welcoming *berghotel* at Trift stands within a beautiful grassy hanging valley surrounded by a bowl of higher peaks. The route is accessed from the middle of town and works its way up the always-interesting gorge with ever-grander views emerging as height is gained.

The main descent described here reverses the outward route (recommended after a long lunch). Or if you prefer, you can take one of the alternative but harder paths to make a circular route.

From the church in the centre of Zermatt turn south and after 100 metres turn right onto Schälpmattgasse. After a further 150 metres turn right again onto a path leading out of the village and across pastures. After 15min turn right again towards the Trift gorge, and after 30min you will reach a **path junction at 1800m** just above a bridge (where the alternative ascent joins) crossing from the other side of the **Triftbach** stream. ◀

From here on the climb passes through the gorge.

Alternatively, this point on the route can be accessed from the main street nearer the station. Find the small street called Chrum, 150 metres north of the church. This turns into Triftweg and climbs past chalets. After 15min

The path climbs alongside the Triftbach in the gorge

you leave the town and the path climbs to the bridge over the Triftbach and joins the main route at the 1800m path junction (30min).

Climb steadily, but steeply, as the path threads among large rocks, sometimes close to the stream, to reach Alterhaupt and the **Edelweiss restaurant** (1961m, 1hr 5min).

In summer 2019 a **raging torrent** of water and mud rushed down the gorge causing significant damage and alarm in the town. It was caused by the sudden outflow of an underground lake that had formed beneath the Trift glacier following several hot months. Such deluges are becoming increasingly common and dangerous in mountain regions throughout the world. In this case the route was quickly repaired, but it is likely that the path will require further work in the future.

From the Edelweiss Restaurant continue up, at first on a gentle incline, through a lightly wooded area that becomes steeper, keeping close to the stream for a while. Climb away from the stream to surmount a large rock, then return to the stream to pass water flow control installations and cross the Triftbach to climb onto the north bank. About 100m below the *berghotel*, you will spot the Swiss flag encouraging you onwards and upwards before you arrive at the **Hotel du Trift** (2337m, 2hr 15min).

The **Hotel du Trift** (2337m) was built in 1900 in the same style as an earlier hotel that was destroyed by a huge avalanche in 1898. It has changed little over the years. It has space for 19 in rooms and 30 in the dormitory. It's a classic example of the old-style

The welcoming Trift hotel

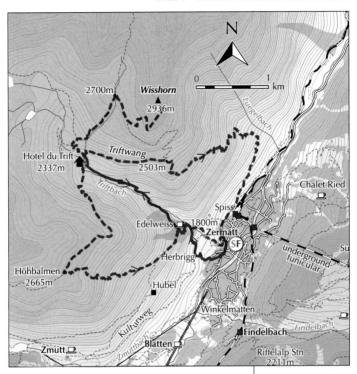

mountain inns developed for the tourists of the Victorian era, but it now serves a modern clientele with elegance and wit. Lunch and an overnight stay are recommended.

To return to Zermatt reverse the ascent path, which takes 1hr 45min into **Zermatt**, after taking the opportunity to refuel at the **Edelweiss** restaurant.

Other options from Trift
There are several options from Trift; these routes are Grade 3 walks involving long descents on steep mountainside paths.

- Descend via the Triftwang–Spiss path into Zermatt (2hr 30min)
- Climb to Höhbalmen and return to Edelweiss on a steep path before dropping into Zermatt (3hr)
- Make an excursion to climb the Wisshorn, 2936m (3hr out and back from Trift, plus the descent)

For the Triftwang–Spiss descent, walk past the hotel, turning right and then right again after 5min. The path climbs and then turns east along the hillside, with tremendous views, climbing gradually to a high point and junction at **2503m**. Descend through avalanche protection to reach the open mountainside. Traverse north towards the **Luegelbach** stream and descend alongside it before turning towards Zermatt and entering the town near the **Spiss** area, passing above the station and continuing into **Zermatt** town centre through the backstreets (2hr 30min).

For the Höhbalmen–Alterhaupt (Edelweiss) route, climb left from the hotel to the Höhbalmen 'ledge', which has extensive views of all the Zermatt peaks, especially the Matterhorn. At the **Höhbalmen path junction** (2665m, 1hr 10min) turn left and descend a good but steep path back to the **Edelweiss** (2hr 20min) and then reverse the initial ascent route into **Zermatt** (3hr).

For the Wisshorn route, follow signs for the Mettelhorn. After climbing for 1hr, turn right at a path junction at about **2700m** and traverse for 500 metres. Take a left turn and climb to two small buildings (one for sheep, the other presumably for their handlers). At this point the route to the 2936m **Wisshorn** summit is clear, passing up a broad ridge with some serious avalanche protection on either side. It's a strange place and steeper than it looks. The summit views are excellent. You can descend the same way you came up, or at the two buildings turn left and drop down through a line of avalanche protection to join the Spiss descent near the **2503m** junction. The direct descent to **Zermatt** via the hotel is preferable (3hr round trip to the Wisshorn plus 1hr 40min descent to Zermatt).

WALK 2

Ascent of the Mettelhorn and Platthorn from Trift

Start	Trift, 2337m
Alternative start	Zermatt, 1620m
Finish	Zermatt, 1620m
Distance	14.5km (18.5km from Zermatt)
Total ascent	1280m (2000m from Zermatt)
Total descent	2000m
Grade	4
Time	7hr 30min (9hr 45min from Zermatt)
Max altitude	Mettelhorn summit, 3406m; Platthorn, 3345m
Refreshments	Hotel du Trift, Edelweiss restaurant at Alterhaupt on the descent
Warning	The short névé and glacier section requires crampons all season. If there is snow on the glacier and summit sections of the route, an ice axe will be needed – check with the Hotel du Trift.

This is certainly the best summit walk in the Zermatt region: a fine day out that takes walking as far as it can go without becoming mountaineering. The summit of the Mettelhorn is a magnificent viewpoint over the entire valley, taking in the sharp ridges of the nearby 4506m Weisshorn and across to the Dom and Täschhorn and north to the Bernese Oberland. The Zinalrothorn and Ober Gabelhorn are close by to the west.

This long, high walk has three sections that require care: a scree approach to the Furggji col; a short section higher on the glacier approach to the Mettelhorn, which is likely to be icy; and the final steep pull to Mettelhorn's sharp, rocky summit.

The route also climbs the Platthorn, which needs no special equipment, although the final climb to the summit may be an even steeper climb than that of the Mettelhorn. The full route described here climbs both peaks – if the Mettelhorn is omitted the route will be 1hr shorter.

The route starts from the Hotel du Trift, saving the 2hr climb from Zermatt and allowing an overnight in this famous mountain hotel. It is possible to do the full route from Zermatt in a single day – but at around 10hr walking with 2000m of ascent and descent, this would be only for the very tough walker.

Ascent from Zermatt

Climb from Zermatt up the Trift gorge to the **Edelweiss** restaurant and then on to the **Hotel du Trift** (2337m). See Walk 1 for a fuller description. The climb takes 2hr 15min.

From the Hotel du Trift, take the path north, signed to the Mettelhorn and Rothornhütte. After 15min of climbing gentle loops, the path to the Rothornhütte turns left (2452m). Turn right here and start to climb more steeply alongside a tumbling stream to a path junction at **2700m** (1hr), where the alpine blue path starts and a path to the Wisshorn heads away to the right. Continue on the alpine path, initially a broad path on grassy hillside until it reaches 2900m where it steepens as it enters white scree (1hr 30min).

Looking down from the summit of the Mettelhorn on the small glacier, the Furggji col and the Platthornl

The route across the scree varies depending on the conditions, so keep an eye out for the current track. Part way across you will cross a deep, but likely dry, channel gouged by water. This may be awkward but head up

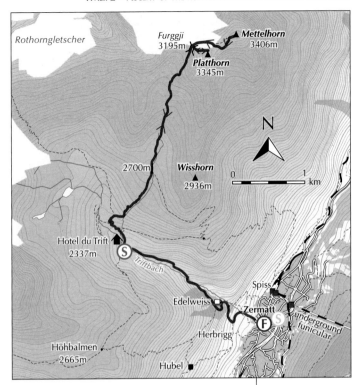

or down to the nearest suitable crossing point. Continue across the sloping scree on thin paths to emerge at the 3195m **Furggji** col by a signpost indicating the routes to the Mettelhorn and Platthorn (2hr 20min). ▸

For the Mettelhorn continue ahead across the *névé* or glacier. It's easy going at first on what is usually a good track, but it then steepens slightly on ice and an occasional glacial lake before the next saddle (3270m). Crampons should be worn. The crossing should take around 15–20min.

From the saddle a clear path zigzags to the sharp summit of the **Mettelhorn**, which has room for three. It

If you are doing both summits, it is best to do the Mettelhorn first as it is further and higher. If you are just doing the Platthorn, turn right at the col.

If snow-covered this would require mountaineering skills and an ice axe.

is capped by rocks, so take care as you scramble the final 20m (3406m, 3hr 20min). This section is steep, but in good conditions should hold few fears. ◄

The **Mettelhorn** has long been a favourite peak for walkers and climbers. Described in Baedeker's 19th-century guides as 'interesting but toilsome', its heritage as a summit to bag goes back many years. The Weisshorn is close at hand and the cross-valley views to the Dom and Täschhorn are tremendous. The Zinalrothorn and Ober Gabelhorn are laid out for inspection, and the Monte Rosa range and peaks towards the Matterhorn dominate to the south.

Reverse the route back down to the Furggji col (40min).

For the Platthorn climb the rocky and unmarked path to the summit directly above the Furggji col. Follow the traces of path with care. If anything, this is a steeper ascent than the Mettelhorn. Reach the **Platthorn** summit (3345m, 25min from the col). ◄ Descend with care by the same route to the **Furggji col**. (The Platthorn ascent and descent takes 40min.)

The views from the Platthorn are impressive, and it is a worthy objective if you don't want to cross the glacier.

Reverse your route back to the **Hotel du Trift** (1hr 50min from Furggji), then take the Trift gorge path down to **Zermatt**, which takes a further 1hr 40min, with the Edelweiss restaurant halfway if further sustenance is required.

WALK 3
*Two-day expedition – Schönbielhütte
via Höhbalmen*

Start/finish	Zermatt, 1620m
Distance	Day 1: 15.5km; Day 2: 13km; total 28.5km
Total ascent	Day 1: 1520m; Day 2: 140m; total 1660m
Total descent	Day 1: 440m; Day 2: 1220m; total 1660m
Grade	3
Time	Day 1: 6hr 30min; Day 2: 3hr 30min; total 10hr
Max altitude	Schönbielhütte, 2694m
Refreshments	Edelweiss restaurant, Hotel du Trift, Schönbielhütte and restaurants in Zmutt on the descent

This two-day walk takes in the Höhbalmen shelf high above Zermatt and Zmutt, providing spectacular views across the Zmutt valley to the north face of the Matterhorn. After climbing the Trift gorge, the route heads over the Höhbalmen plateau before traversing below the Ober Gabelhorn, descending to the upper Zmutt valley and making a final climb to the Schönbielhütte. The following day, after you have spent a night in the hut, the walk returns to Zermatt by a valley route.

The route can be done in a single day, but this is likely to require a ten-hour walk (plus extra time) and forgoes the opportunity to stay in this spectacularly located and welcoming mountain hut. The challenges of the route include the amount of ascent needed on the first day and the path that traverses under the various Gabelhorns, which might feel exposed to some walkers; it can be tricky in snowy and icy conditions, in which case take crampons.

The essence of the route is the amazing views of the Matterhorn and indeed all the peaks of the Zermatt valley between Höhbalmen and Schöenbiel.

Day 1
From the church in the centre of Zermatt head south, turning right after 100 metres on to Schälpmattgasse.

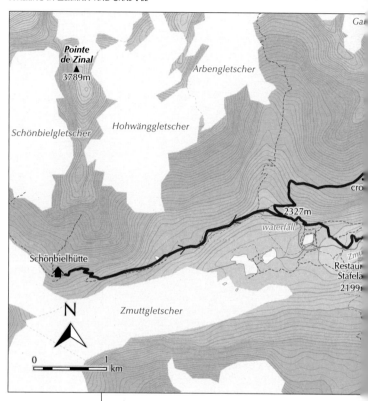

The passage along the Trift gorge is always interesting and a contrast with the open mountainsides to come.

After 150 metres turn right onto a path heading out of town and after 15min turn right towards the Trift gorge. Climb steadily to reach the **Edelweiss** restaurant in just under 1hr. Continue on up the gorge to reach the **Hotel du Trift** in 2hr 15min (see Walk 1). ◄

From the hotel at Trift, take the left turn immediately behind the hotel. This briefly crosses a flat valley area and then climbs the steep-looking but actually reasonably graded path across the Litxinen hillside to the south. As you emerge onto the crest, you will be greeted by the Matterhorn in one of the most dramatic sights Zermatt

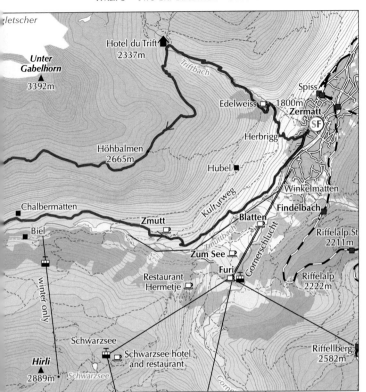

has to offer. Continue, to arrive at the **Höhbalmen path junction** (2665m, 3hr 15min) 1hr after leaving Trift.

The broad grassy plateau continues for some distance. ▸ The 3392m Gabelhorn sits high above the path to the north. The path contours round the hillside and heads west, with the Dent d'Hérens, a difficult 4000m mountain hidden behind the bulk of the Matterhorn, coming into view.

The plateau comes to an end and the path takes a high traverse across the hillside. Evidence of rockfalls and streams washing out the route is met at various

It's a place to spend time, weather allowing, and soak in the views of the 4000m peaks walling the valley.

The Matterhorn dominates the view at Höhbalmen

points. After passing **a cross** (1hr from Höhbalmen), start the descent to the valley, arriving at a path junction at **2327m**, 2hr 45min after leaving Trift.

A path and a track head west; they join later. Take the path and climb very gradually alongside a stream and under moraine and rock outcrops. ◄ Pass a small lake and cross the stream where the track merges, then climb to a second lake. For 400 metres the path follows the moraine crest before climbing the final zigzags to the **Schönbielhütte** (2694m, 6hr 30min).

The moraine of the Zmuttgletscher sits above and the walk through the ablation valley is idyllic.

The **Schönbielhütte** sits on a promontory of rock, facing the Zmutt ridge of the Matterhorn and the Dent d'Hérens. Unseen above is the 4000m Dent Blanche. The hut may be busy with mountaineers making the high-level glacial traverse from Chamonix to Zermatt, for whom it is the final night of a one-week tour. The Zmutt glacier below is not the archetypical clean, white glacier; it is almost entirely covered in stone, appearing more Himalayan than Alpine.

Day 2

Reverse the ascent route only as far as the path junction at **2327m** (1hr 10min). From the junction, follow the path down, which soon starts to zigzag steeply. A spectacular waterfall can be seen on the right. After 15min cross directly over a track and continue through a flatter, lightly wooded area to reach a path junction. (To the right is a bridge crossing the Zmuttbach river.) Continue left and meander downhill, then climb steeply for 50m up out of the river valley. The path now continues past **Chalbermatten** (2105m), reaching **Zmutt** in 5km (1936m, 2hr 30min).

> **Zmutt** is a tiny alp hamlet mostly taken over by restaurants. It enjoys good, if somewhat low and limited, views of the Matterhorn.

> From Zmutt the most direct route to Zermatt is to leave the village on the broad path heading east, then continue downhill, ignoring all paths to the left and right. This is a popular path and soon leads down past the main cable car station (to Furi and Schwarzsee) and on into the centre of **Zermatt** (3hr 30min).

The Schönbielhütte is set on a small plateau high above the moraine

WALK 4

The villages of Zmutt,
Zum See and Blatten

Start/finish	Zermatt, 1620m
Distance	7.5km
Total ascent/descent	360m
Grade	1
Time	2hr–2hr 30min
Max altitude	1936m at Zmutt
Refreshments	Zermatt, Zum See, Blatten
Note	The cable car to Furi can be used to shorten the walk, removing nearly 300m of ascent or descent if desired.

This is justifiably a popular route, following a well-graded old mule track to the tiny alp hamlet of Zmutt, where ample refreshment opportunities are available. The Matterhorn is visible, at least in part, for much of the time, while views up to the head of the valley are also spectacular. The return to Zermatt can be made in a variety of ways, either by retracing the ascent route, or, as described in this walk, by visiting the tiny alp hamlets of Zum See and Blatten, both of which have popular restaurants and views down to Zermatt and across towards Riffelalp and Riffelberg, making an interesting and leisurely circular route.

From the church at the southern end of the main street, walk south in the direction of the large Furi/Schwarzsee cable car station, forking right to follow a track indicated by a yellow diamond waymark (15min). After a further 10min, fork right once again to follow an old mule track on a steady uphill gradient. The route climbs up easily through lightly wooded hillside and meadows, shaded by a mixture of pine and larch trees, to reach a junction of several paths at a collection of chalets. Continue ahead, with the hamlet now in view, to arrive in **Zmutt** (1936m, 1hr).

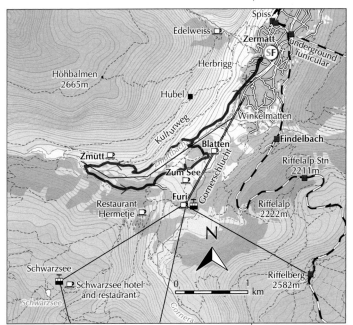

Zmutt is a tiny collection of chalets and alpine buildings with a small hotel and restaurant that seem to take over much of the rest of the centre. Several late medieval houses and farm buildings, dating from the 14th and 15th centuries, surround the simple white chapel. Zmutt is one of the earliest inhabited settlements in Switzerland.

From the centre take the broad path signed to Furi and descend to cross a wooden bridge over the **Zmuttbach** gorge, then climb to the small tarmac road and turn left to begin the return to Zermatt. After 30min you will reach a junction of paths and tracks. Ahead leads directly to Furi, while a path to the left descends, at times fairly steeply, through woods to reach the charming little village of **Zum See** with its welcoming restaurant (1766m, 1hr 45min).

Looking back at Zum See from Blatten

From the centre of Zum See retrace the final 30 metres of path used to enter the village, then at the path junction turn left and follow the path down across a meadow to **Blatten**, which can be seen below, where another popular restaurant with fine views awaits (1738m). Walk up to the little white chapel and then turn left into woods, descending gently and passing 'fitness trail' apparatus. Cross the Zmuttbach stream, then 2min later turn right to join the main path, retracing the ascent route down to **Zermatt** (2hr–2hr 30min).

WALK 5

Balcony route to Zmutt and the Kulturweg

Start/finish	Zermatt, 1620m
Distance	9km
Total ascent/descent	460m
Grade	2
Time	3hr 45min
Max altitude	2120m
Refreshments	Zmutt

This is a superb walk on good paths with spectacular views to the east towards Riffelberg and to the south towards the icy peaks of the Breithorn, Castor, Pollux, Liskamm and Monte Rosa, with the Matterhorn providing striking views for much of the way. The return to Zermatt from Zmutt follows the signed Kulturweg route, which highlights various points of interest and unusual buildings, including a barn dating from the early 13th century, claimed to be the oldest in Switzerland.

From the church at the southern end of the main street in Zermatt turn south and walk in the direction of the Matterhorn for 1min, then turn right onto Schälpstrasse, signed to Herbrigg, Hubel, Zmutt, and the Kulturweg. The cobbled path passes between gardens and chalets. At the next sign turn right (the way ahead is a dead end). Now climb up steeply next to and across a meadow and

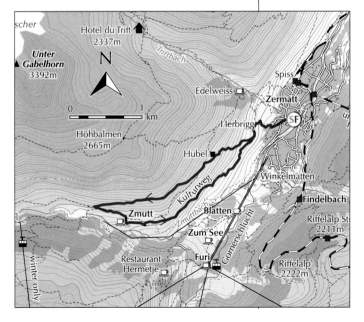

turn left, signed to Hubel and Zmutt. Climb to **Herbrigg** (1750m, 25min). Keep right at the path junction and climb through chalets, passing numerous old barns at 1880m, and continue up to **Hubel**, a small group of farm chalets high above Zermatt (1950m, 50min).

Continue for 3min, then fork right to take the higher path signed to Zmutt (you can take the fork to the left if you prefer a lower descent to Zmutt, but the views are less spectacular). The path steepens, with broadening views towards the Breithorn, and then the Matterhorn comes into view. Continue skirting the hillside to a high point (2120m) and a gate to enjoy superb views; the Matterhorn dominates the scene, and Zmutt can be seen far below. The path now descends, gently at first, then a little steeper, as it approaches the junction with the main valley path near the dam. Turn left to join the main path, then 10min later turn right to drop down into the village of **Zmutt** (1936m, 1hr 40min).

Follow the **Kulturweg**, signed from the centre of Zmutt, on a broad smooth path down the valley for 200

Old barns at Herbrigg on the Kulturweg

metres, then turn sharply left by a chalet and immediately right up next to a rock slab. The path is now clearly marked, passing old barns and chalets, as well as stone cattle pens, with plenty of information boards to enlighten passers-by. ▸

Undulating across a steep hillside, the route offers good views down to Zermatt and across the valley. Eventually, you will start to descend steeply on the path by the meadow, used on the initial ascent, to arrive on the outskirts of Zermatt. Turn left, walk down the cobbled path to meet the main path into the town, then turn left and you will arrive back at the church.

One incredibly old barn at Herbrigg, dating from the 13th century, is considered to be the oldest in the Alps.

The **Kulturweg** is a waymarked route visiting some of the oldest buildings and farming features of the Zermatt region, with 14 information boards in several languages along the way. Highlights include a huge barn or 'Metzgasse' built in 1853, measuring 15 metres in width, and a barn dating from 1261, which is believed to be the oldest in the Alps, if not the whole of Europe; most of the wood dates from 1313, although some dates back to a previous building from 1145. More detailed information on these and other features, including animal pens and a lynx trap, can be found at www.kulturweg-zermatt.ch.

WALK 6

*Zermatt to Sunnegga –
the Findeln villages*

Start	Zermatt, 1620m
Finish	Sunnegga, 2288m
Distance	6km
Total ascent	670m
Grade	1
Time	2hr
Max altitude	Sunnegga, 2288m
Refreshments	Bakery and restaurant in Winkelmatten; several restaurants in Findeln, Sunnegga
Note	From Sunnegga this route links with Walk 14 (descending from Sunnegga) and Walk 15, which explores higher up the mountain.

Although it is all uphill, this is an easy route. The path is well made, well graded and presents no problems. The star attraction, in addition to the views, is the Findelbach valley and several old hamlets that make up Findeln, which is now populated with a number of restaurants, providing a culinary trail. The best brownie known to man is served in one; after the climb you may feel you have earned it. From Sunnegga either retrace the ascent route, return to Zermatt in the funicular or follow Walk 14 back to Zermatt via Chalet Ried. Alternatively, you could follow Walk 15 and explore further up the mountain.

From the church in the centre of Zermatt, cross the river, then turn right and head uphill through chalets on the lightly signed footpath to **Winkelmatten**. Turn left at Winkelmatten church and climb up a straight road that turns left and becomes a path. Climb up to the railway line and then cross it (20min).

The path climbs on ideally graded zigzags, gaining height easily and quickly. Thirty minutes after crossing the railway, keep right at a junction. The route follows

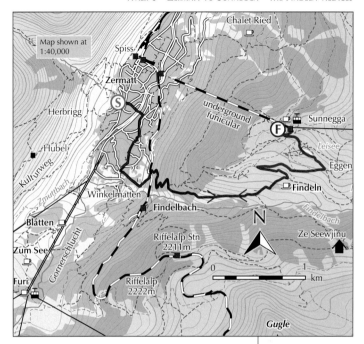

signs to Findeln zu gasse, the larger of the hamlets. The path straightens as it climbs above the **Findelbach**, passing old barns and climbing easily into **Findeln** to reach the first of several restaurants (2051m, 1hr 15min).

Continue to a second hamlet, 5min further uphill, where there is another restaurant, and then on to the hamlet of **Eggen** (2177m). Eggen also has a fine restaurant. Several paths and tracks lead to Sunnegga, but the recommended route is the path up from Eggen. It's less than 30min to Sunnegga, but it is perhaps the steepest part of the walk. The path leads to just below the station building. Climb the final few metres into the **Sunnegga** complex (2288m, 2hr). Either return to Zermatt in the funicular or take one of the other options mentioned below.

Other options

From Sunnegga several onward routes are possible: Walk 15 heads towards Tufteren and climbs to the higher station of Blauherd, while Walk 14 continues the culinary theme, descending to Zermatt via further eating opportunities at the Adler restaurant at Findeln Wildi and in Ried.

WALK 7

Gletschergarten and Gorner gorge walk

Start	Furi cable car station, 1867m
Finish	Zermatt bottom cable car station, 1615m
Alternative finish	Furi cable car station
Distance	6.5km
Total ascent	180m
Total descent	420m
Grade	1–2
Time	2hr minimum
Max altitude	2000m
Refreshments	Furi
Access	Cable car to Furi
Note	This route can be shortened by starting and finishing at Furi, although this would leave out the Gorner gorge (Gornerschlucht) walk.
Warning	If taking small children on this route make sure they are well supervised. The route crosses a suspension bridge, and the walkways in the Gletschergarten can be difficult to negotiate for very small people. The walkways in the gorge are very well constructed and safe, but there are many steps.

This is a fantastic outing for adults and children alike. The route takes in some of the rocks and rock formations left by the subglacial streams in the Gletschergarten, with plenty of information boards to assist your understanding, followed by an exploration of the spectacular Gorner gorge before returning to Zermatt. (A charge is made for the gorge walk, currently CHF5 for adults.)

The route passes a children's adventure playground and picnic/ BBQ area, an exciting – but very safe – suspension bridge, as well as all manner of interesting rock formations, including a small cave in the Gletschergarten that can be explored. Allow at least an extra half-hour for the Gletschergarten, plus additional time in the gorge for the inevitable multitude of photographs! It would not be excessive to allow most of a day, particularly if taking young children.

From the Furi cable car station walk down to Restaurant Furi and turn left on a small path signed for the Gletschergarten. Climb between chalets and past Les Marmottes restaurant, then continue up a grassy piste

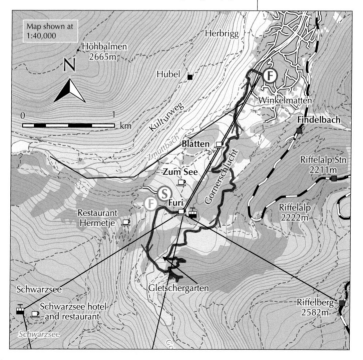

and through a lightly wooded area. After 10–12min take a path that branches left on a wooden boardwalk, then climb a little further to reach the suspension bridge across the upper Gorner gorge. Cross the bridge and continue into a children's adventure play area, with picnic and BBQ facilities. Walk through this area and turn left, rising to a track. Now turn right signed to the **Gletschergarten** and enter through the gate.

> Information boards in the **Gletschergarten** detail the rocks and rock formations that can be seen, with a suggested route that will include all the features. As well as interesting rock formations, there

Walkway in the spectacular Gornerschlucht

is a small cave – the site of an old soap stone mine. Allow at least 30min.

Rejoin the track and descend to reach a path junction in front of the Riffelberg bottom gondola station near **Furi** (20min from the Gletschergarten). ▶ If you want to return to Furi from the bottom of the track, turn left and climb to the station (10min).

To continue to the gorge, turn right and pass under the **Riffelberg gondola**, then pass Restaurant Alm and 5min later take a path down to the left, signed 'Winkelmatten and Zermatt'. Descend through woods to meet a track. Turn right, then fork left on another path signed to Blatten and Zermatt. Descend on this smooth path for 4min, then turn sharp right before the bridge onto another path signed **'Gornerschlucht'**. For the first few minutes it's only possible to hear the roar of the water far below, as you can't see into the gorge at this point. After 8–10min all this changes. Turn left to drop down into the gorge, first on a path then down about 100 wooden steps, following a series of wooden walkways and platforms with awe-inspiring views down through narrow clefts in the rock to the gushing water below.

Emerge from the gorge path and turn right, initially down a ski piste, onto a path leading directly past some sports facilities to the bottom cable car station, with the centre of **Zermatt** beyond.

The track is quite rough and less interesting, so you might prefer to return via the suspension bridge.

WALK 8
Schwarzsee and Stafelalp –
under the Matterhorn

Start/finish	Zermatt, 1620m
Distance	16.5km
Total ascent/descent	1030m
Grade	3
Time	5hr 30min
Max altitude	Schwarzsee, 2583m
Refreshments	Mountain restaurants at Blatten, Zum See, Hermetje, Schwarzsee, Stafelalp and Zmutt

With the Matterhorn rising sharply above, Schwarzsee is one of the great viewpoints of the Alps. Views stretch round the full Monte Rosa range to the east and towards the Dent Blanche and mountains on the west of the Mattertal, which rise above the Zmutt valley. Towards the north the Dom and Täschhorn dominate the horizon. It's a justifiably popular area, but even the visitors disappear quickly in the vastness of the scene, with some twenty 4000m peaks to see. You could, of course, take a cable car from Zermatt to Schwarzsee, but earning the view only enriches it. You are likely to find yourself in the company of mountaineers on their way to the Matterhorn in search of great and hopefully successful adventures.

With no route-finding or path difficulties to speak of, this is a straightforward route with coffee, lunch and cake options throughout. The route is also fine done in reverse, although the track up from Stafel to Schwarzsee would be a bit of a slog in the hot midday sun. You could take the lift down to Zermatt to save your knees.

From the church at the southern end of the main street in Zermatt head south and pass the bottom cable car station (10min). Begin to climb on a good path to the right of the **Zmuttbach** stream and take the first left turn (20min). Drop down briefly and cross a small stream, then start the climb, initially on steps, past chalets under the cable

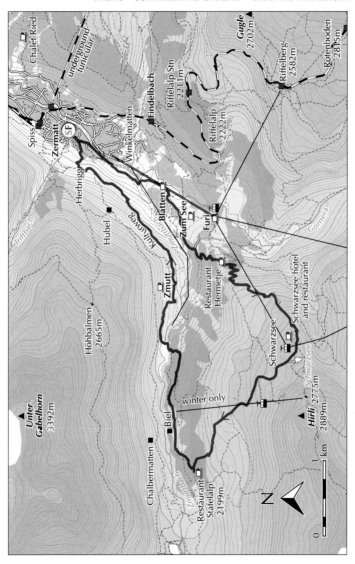

Both hamlets have restaurants if early sustenance is needed.

car line and past Blatten's chapel, continuing through the hamlet of **Blatten** to reach **Zum See**. ◄

Keep climbing, passing – but not taking – signs to the cable car station at Furi (45min). The path now heads away from the cable car line. Cross a track and then after 100 metres cross another. Climb steeply in the woods to reach **Restaurant Hermetje** (2053m, 1hr 30min). ◄ Keep right at a turn above the restaurant.

This is a great viewpoint, with Zermatt beginning to look small in the valley below and the Breithorn showing its stern north face above.

The path climbs up the lightly wooded hillside, which allows light and breezes to penetrate while protecting you from the sun. The path makes innumerable zigzags, and after 2220m you will leave the trees behind and soon get your first glimpse of the top of the Matterhorn. Pass under the cable car line at 2324m (2hr 30min). The path continues to zigzag, although relenting a little. Turn a corner at 2400m and climb the crest of a moraine that leads directly to the cable car station, hotel and restaurant at **Schwarzsee** (2583m, 3hr 15min).

> **Schwarzsee** has a long history in Alpine exploration. Early Matterhorn climbs began here, and in the 1950s and 1960s it was a popular camping spot for the impecunious hard men at the forefront of climbing. We will never know, and can only imagine, what they would have thought of the CHF150 nightly charge at the hotel. Or what they would have made of the CHF1.25 per pound exchange rate compared with the CHF10 per pound rate back then. There is a small chapel by the lake, which is a 200-metre walk further on.

Take the broad track descending north-west. After 25min, at 2380m, take a right-hand turn that drops over pastures then into woods, directly to **Restaurant Stafelalp** (2199m, 4hr)

From Restaurant Stafelalp there are many options on both sides of the Zmuttbach stream. Find the signed path below the restaurant and follow this. At first it is a path but then becomes a track. The walk then turns left

and descends on a path to the remote hamlet of Stafel and then turns right on a track to the delightful, postcard-perfect hamlet of **Biel**.

From here there is a choice of upper or lower tracks, both of which meet at the southern end of the Zmuttbach dam wall; take the upper track, then keep right at the small winter ski station and just before a somewhat unexpected electricity booster station, turn left and descend steeply to the side of the dam. Turn right and then left to cross the dam wall and climb to join the path on the north side of the valley, then turn right to drop down into welcoming **Zmutt** (1936m, 4hr 45min).

From Zmutt the path options multiply yet again. The simplest and quickest option (it has after all been a fairly long day) is to stay on the main path, descending directly to **Zermatt** in around 45min (5hr 30min).

Other descent options

Other descent options from Zmutt are explored in Walks 4 and 5. Perhaps the easiest of these is the Kulturweg (Walk 4), which stays high in woods before dropping sharply into Zermatt. It is much less walked and has the added attraction of passing Europe's oldest known barn.

Wayside refreshments near the hamlet of Biel in the Zmutt valley

WALK 9
Schwarzsee to the Hörnlihütte

Start/finish	Schwarzsee, 2583m
Distance	8km
Total ascent/descent	720m
Grade	3–4
Time	4hr
Max altitude	3260m, at the Hörnlihütte
Refreshments	Schwarzsee and the Hörnlihütte
Access	By cable car to Schwarzsee
Warning	Although much frequented by all levels of walkers, this high mountain route requires care. If you don't have a head for heights, some parts of the ascent/descent might be challenging.

The Hörnlihütte is embedded deep in climbing myth. It is the start point for the climbs on the 'easier' ridge of the Matterhorn, a place where dreams come true and where hopes are dashed. The walk to the start of the climb, however, is quite sufficient for most people.

The walk follows a well-made path, which in places passes through very steep terrain with long drops. Occasionally the path is less than one metre wide, but if you stick to the path, there is little to worry about. Be prepared to queue at a few ladders and other choke points and wait while walkers pass in the other direction. Pick a fine day, both for safety and the views, and ensure you are fit and acclimatised at 3000m. It is busier at weekends, so if possible do this route on a weekday.

From the Schwarzsee cable car and hotel, drop down a few metres towards the Schwarzsee (Black Lake) and pass above its southern side, where there are wonderful views of the lake, a small chapel and Ober Gabelhorn beyond. Start to climb on a good but rocky path that passes steeply over a ledge and then levels out across an unexpected and ugly piste. Continue over another rise before arriving at the **Hirli lift station** (2775m, 40min), the turn for the Glacier Path (see Walk 10).

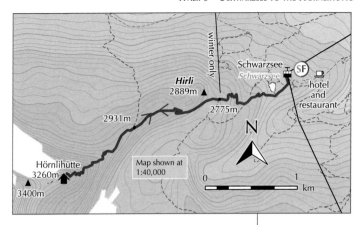

At Hirli you meet the first big obstacle: the high brown cliff that can be clearly seen from the valley. The path skirts to the left and then turns around the cliff on metal walkways, before climbing on sloping paths, which some may find a little awkward, to reach a rocky ridge (50min). If you are in doubt about the route and have found it too much so far, it may be wise to return. But if the first section went well, be assured that the rest of the route is no more exposed than what you have already done.

The next stage is perhaps the biggest surprise. Having breached the wall of cliffs, the route becomes a gentle walk over sloping ground for the next 15min. At **2931m** a path joins from Stafel in the Zmutt valley (1hr 10min) and ahead you will see a rock pyramid – your walkers' summit – rising above.

From here on the path is nearly always a broad, rocky walkway cut into the mountain. In places chains and ropes are provided, and a series of ladders will provide a proper test for the lungs. ▸ The ladders are two-way, so keep to one side and leave the other side clear for those descending. After 30–40min of this, you will pass a large rock (a *gendarme* in climbing parlance) then turn a corner 100m below the hut, which you will spot for the first time since starting the final climb. From here the path

Watch out for descending parties and plan to meet at the least inconvenient spot, if you can.

75

*The good path
climbs the rock
steps towards the
Hörnlihütte*

Actual times will
vary considerably
depending on
experience,
acclimatisation and
traffic conditions.

is easier, and you will arrive at the **Hörnlihütte** after 2hr 15min. ◄

The first **Hörnli Hut** was built in 1880 and had 17 beds. In 1911 the main white building (the Belvedere mountain hotel) was built by the civic community of Zermatt. Both the hut and the Belvedere mountain hotel have been expanded over the decades, with the most recent extension in 2013–14 providing a total of 170 places. The current hut has viewing windows and is positioned right at the start of the climb.

The descent may be easier or harder depending on how heights affect you. Again, make space for those ascending. You are likely to complete the steep section in 50min, reaching Hirli in 1hr 20min and Schwarzsee in 1hr 45min.

WALK 10
The Matterhorn Glacier Trail

Start	Schwarzsee, 2583m
Finish	Trockener Steg, 2939m
Alternative finish	Schwarzsee, 2583m
Distance	6.5km (11.5km to Schwarzsee)
Total ascent	550m (700m to Schwarzsee)
Total descent	200m (700m to Schwarzsee)
Grade	2
Time	2hr 30min; Schwarzsee 4hr
Max altitude	2925m on the trail after the Theodulgletschersee
Refreshments	Trockener Steg and Schwarzsee only
Warning	Best avoided in bad weather, as route finding would be difficult and you won't see anything.

The Matterhorn Glacier Trail connects two high cable car stations, taking you to the very edge of the Theodul and Furgg glaciers beneath the mighty Matterhorn. Although it is high (2800m), and stony underfoot as you cross the debris of glaciers, the route is not difficult.

The trail is clearly waymarked by paint markers on rocks and some marker posts, route finding might prove challenging in a landscape with few features if the cloud comes down. What's more, not being able to see the glaciers and surrounding mountains due to bad weather would be very disappointing.

This route could be done in either direction. Starting from Schwarzsee, as recommended here, is slightly longer and has more ascent, but you are rewarded with views of the Matterhorn and later the Monte Rosa range and the whole set of Zermatt peaks. A start from Trockener Steg involves 350m less ascent, is slightly easier to follow and is also quicker, but in this direction the views are of the Matterhorn and little else. For some the deciding factor will be walking away from Trockener Steg, which is understandable: it's a large and unattractive cable car station.

For those who would prefer to walk back down to Schwarzsee, a variant is described.

From Schwarzsee take the path signed towards the Hörnlihütte and drop down, passing above the southern side of the lake, a very photogenic spot, and then begin to climb up. Continue over one rise, then cross a piste and then climb up another rise before coming to the **Hirli** cable car top station (2775m, 40min).

Turn left and drop down, initially gently, then steeply, into a glacial bowl on a very stony path. Shortly after a red marker pole, at 2700m, cross a bridge over a stream of glacial meltwater. Skirt the moraine, either at the bottom or slightly on it, and seek out a critical left turn marked only by paint splashes (2700m, 1hr). Take some care as this is easy to miss. ◄

The scene is vast. The stony ground vacated by glaciers gives way to the Furgggletscher above, and higher still the bulk of the Matterhorn looms.

From here climb steadily. The path may be unclear in places, so keep an eye on the painted waymarks. Pass boards explaining the geology and glaciation of the area in several languages (including English). After 1hr 30min pass the first small lake, **Furggsee**, 2874m, and continue to climb towards an undulating plateau.

This **plateau** is another photogenic spot, with the Monte Rosa and its surrounding peaks ahead; the Mischabel peaks, which Zermatt shares with Saas-Fee, to the left; and further to the left the Weisshorn, Zinalrothorn, Ober Gabelhorn and Dent Blanche, which are shared with the valleys to the west. Behind is the east face of the Matterhorn, framed by the Hörnli and Furgg ridges.

Press on over more level ground to reach an area of red rocks, their iron content clear to see, and drop down. At a yellow signpost (the first since Hirli) you will see the bulk and cable of Trockener Steg. Descend to the north of **Theodulgletschersee** and climb the 50m up to the **Trockener Steg station** (2939m).

Variant descent to Schwarzsee

If you want to avoid a cable car descent from Trockener Steg to Schwarzsee, take the path signed to Schwarzsee. The signs claim 1hr 45min, which is perhaps generous.

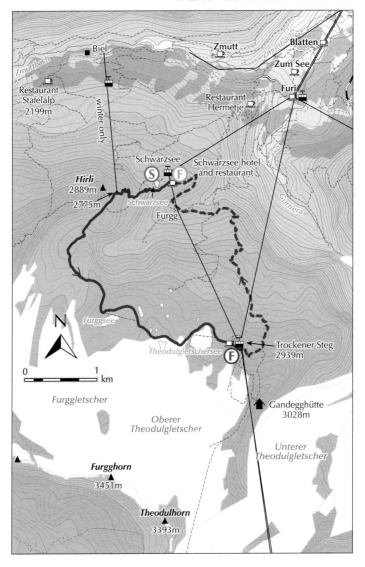

The path passes lakes on the rocky glacial remains en route to Trockener Steg

The good path – sometimes referred to as the *saumweg* or mule track – drops down through rocky bands, passes under the **cable car line** from Furi to Trockener Steg (not generally in use in the summer) and comes out on a grassy hillside. Pass a turn, where a direct descent to Furi is possible, then drop down to pass by the cable car line at **Furgg**, before climbing up a steady track towards Schwarzsee, 150m higher. Turn left and you will soon reach the **restaurant and cable car at Schwarzsee** (2583m, 1hr 30min). Keep an eye on the time as the last cable car descent in July and August leaves at 1700 (2019 timetable).

WALK 11

Gornergrat to Riffelsee, Riffelberg and Riffelalp

Start	Gornergrat station, 3090m
Finish	Riffelalp station, 2211m
Alternative finish	Riffelberg, 2582m
Distance	6.5km (4.5km to Riffelberg)
Total ascent	40m
Total descent	880m (550m to Riffelberg)
Grade	2
Time	2hr 15min (1hr 30min to Riffelberg)
Max altitude	3100m at Gornergrat
Refreshments	Gornergrat, Riffelberg and Riffelalp
Access	Gornergrat railway
Warning	Altitude can affect anyone and at any time, but especially if you have only recently arrived in the Alps. This walk begins at over 3000m, so be prepared to feel slightly less energetic.

A ride on the mountain railway to Gornergrat is one of the highlights of any trip to Zermatt, for walkers, tourists and mountaineers alike. The views are spectacular towards the frontier peaks of Monte Rosa, Liskamm, Castor, Pollux and the Breithorn, not to mention the dominating Matterhorn and the Gorner glacier below.

The route is described here as a descent route because the best views of the Matterhorn and neighbouring peaks can be appreciated in this direction, with exceptional views of a wild, glacial mountain landscape. The route can be walked in its entirety or in sections, with options to join or rejoin the railway at Gornergrat, Rotenboden, Riffelberg and Riffelalp. Nestling below the Riffelhorn (2928m), Riffelsee and its neighbouring smaller lake are deservedly popular beauty spots; while below the lakes a beautiful, rock-strewn valley provides endless views of the Matterhorn, before contouring easily round the hillside. The descent from Riffelberg is on a good but fairly steep path crossing under a rocky hillside down to the hamlet of Riffelalp, (a well-sited collection of hotels and restaurants), followed by a short level walk (or ride on the tramway) to Riffelalp station. An optional additional walk along the Hohtälligrat ridge, providing yet more exceptional views of the upper Gornergletscher and Monte Rosa, is included.

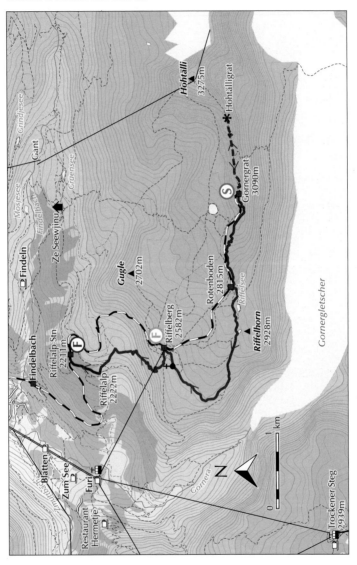

Exploring along the Hohtälligrat ridge

Arriving at Gornergrat station you have two options: either join the throng admiring the views from the terrace before beginning the walk down, or explore the Hohtälligrat ridge. To make an excursion to the ridge, pass behind the huge hotel and restaurant building to reach a series of viewing platforms. A hiking path is signed ahead, marked with the usual red-and-white paint splashes. Pass to the right of a rocky outcrop, then initially descend onto a good broad path that follows the crest of the ridge. ▶

Continue along the ridge, climbing to a high point (3152m, 15–20min). The best views can be found here. The onward route to the Hohtälli cable car station detracts from rather than adds to the route, so turn around at this point and return to Gornergrat station.

Views towards the Monte Rosa are exceptional and well worth the ridge walk.

From the terrace by Gornergrat station take a broad, rough track that drops to the left, and then at the first signpost, signed to Rotenboden, bear left. Various interlacing paths all make their way down the rocky hillside, but follow the main track, which is clear, to arrive at a path junction for Riffelsee, seen below, and a path to nearby **Rotenboden** station, rising to the right (2815m, 40–45min).

Take the track down to **Riffelsee**. Walk around either side of the lake, as there are good views and the possibility of a perfect reflection of the Matterhorn if there is no wind. Continue down to another smaller lake and at the next path junction keep left, signed 40min to Riffelberg (the path to the right is a shorter but less interesting route). Five minutes later fork left again, now signed 35min to Riffelberg (the path to the right is a shorter route that undulates but which is predominantly downhill) and descend into a beautiful boulder-strewn valley with the Matterhorn directly ahead. At the next path junction fork right on a contouring path towards a large prominent post, where a path joins from the left. The path climbs a slope then eases round the hillside, with superb views across the valley towards the Ober

The Matterhorn above Riffelsee

The onward descent to Riffelberg is on a good but fairly steep path, so if you prefer you could rejoin the railway here.

Gabelhorn and Zinalrothorn, to reach a small chapel. **Riffelberg** can be seen just beyond (2582m, 45min from Rotenboden). ◀

Riffelberg occupies a prominent site and is also a transport hub, with both the Gornergrat railway and a cable car from Furi. There is a large restaurant complex and a small shop at the station, while the Riffelberg Hotel provides more luxurious facilities and accommodation.

From the station descend towards the Riffelberg Hotel (Riffelhaus, 1853), then take the path passing to the left below the hotel terrace. After 2min take the right fork, signed to Riffelalp. Descend steeply through a rocky section, pass under the cable car and descend the hillside in a series of zigzags. After 12–15min the gradient eases a little and Riffelalp appears below. Continue to descend, then cross a stream and descend to meet a track. Turn left and walk down the track to **Riffelalp** (2222m, 50min from Riffelberg). To get to the station walk between the hotel and the restaurant, following the tramway tracks on a level gravel path to arrive at the station (5min).

WALK 12
Riffelalp and a woodland walk to Grüensee

Start/finish	Riffelalp station, 2211m
Distance	7km (8km via the higher track route)
Total ascent/descent	260m
Grade	1
Time	2hr (2hr 15min via higher track route)
Max altitude	2300m at Grüensee, (2370m on higher track route)
Refreshments	Riffelalp, Mountain Lodge Ze Seewjinu
Access	Gornergrat railway

This straightforward, circular route takes in the beautiful scenery of the lightly wooded southern slopes of the Findeln valley and Grüensee lake. If possible begin the walk first thing in the morning, when the water on Grüensee is less likely to be disturbed and at its best for clear reflections of the mountains. The return route to Riffelalp on the slightly higher path is a delight, with the Matterhorn in almost constant view, and it only involves an additional 60m of climbing. An alternative ascent route has been included via a higher track that has the advantage of uninterrupted views across the Findeln valley; however, it is less picturesque in other respects.

Onward walking options are suggested if a full day's outing is planned.

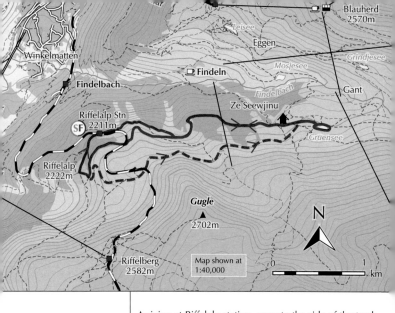

Arriving at Riffelalp station, cross to the side of the track furthest from the station building and turn right to begin the walk, initially on a broad track that crosses a bridge. The track soon becomes a path through open woodland of pine and larch. After 10min you will reach a path junction with a path up to the right, signed to Riffelberg; this is the path to take on the return route. Continue ahead, enjoying glimpses across the valley as the path undulates around the hillside. Pass under cable car lines and climb to emerge on open ground. You will see **Mountain Lodge Ze Seewjinu** ahead. Walk past the restaurant and at a path junction maintain direction for 200 metres to arrive at **Grüensee** (2300m, 1hr).

> **Grüensee** is one of just five lakes in the Findeln valley (see Walk 16), and it is a popular destination for walkers arriving from either Riffelalp or from Sunnegga and Findeln. Allow at least 15 minutes to walk around the lake, to enjoy the different viewpoints and reflections of the surrounding mountains.

Retrace the route to the restaurant and back down the path used on the ascent, keeping left when you pass under the **cable car lines** to take the left fork. Continue for a further 15min to the path junction seen earlier at 2240m, signed to Riffelberg.

Climb the path for around 3min, then maintaining direction cross diagonally over a track and continue to climb for a total of about 60m to reach a high point with views of the Matterhorn ahead. Remaining at this height for a short while enjoy the views through a lightly wooded section before dropping to cross the **Gornergrat railway lines**, then continue downhill to reach a track just above Riffelalp. Turn right and descend to **Riffelalp**, and on to the station to catch the train.

Alternative ascent to Grüensee via the higher track

From the centre of Riffelalp, with the hotel on your left, turn left up the steep track signed to Grüensee. After 20min the track passes under the railway, and a few minutes later a superb, elevated view opens up to the north: the Findeln valley, Sunnegga and Blauherd and the mountains of the Bernese Oberland in the far distance beyond the end of the Mattertal. The track now undulates slightly to reach a high point at 2382m where the track divides (35min). Descend on the left track, with fine views, to reach a track and path junction just to the right and above **Mountain Lodge Ze Seewjinu**. Turn right onto the path and continue for 200 metres to reach **Grüensee** (2300m, 1hr).

Other options from Grüensee

There are a number of options to extend the walk to a full day. The choices are as follows:

- From Grüensee walk back towards Mountain Lodge Ze Seewjinu, taking the path to the right down into the Findeln valley to the small Mosjesee reservoir, then walk up to Eggen and Findeln. This will then link with two routes returning to Zermatt: Walk 6 reversed (Grade 1, 6km, 1hr 30min to 2hr) and Walk 14 via a balcony route and several restaurants (Grade

Morning reflection in Grüensee

1–2, 9km, 2hr). Alternatively, from Findeln climb to Sunnegga for a faster descent on the underground funicular.

- From Grüensee follow Walk 16 in reverse for a tour of the five lakes in the Findeln valley (Grade 2, 9km, 3hr).

- Return to Riffelalp and walk down through woods to Furi, initially taking the path passing just above the Alphitta Restaurant, then passing Restaurant Chämi-Hitta and Restaurant Ritti, dropping steeply to reach the road, with Furi directly ahead (45min from Riffelalp). Turn left to walk up the road to Furi (10min) or turn right to either walk down the road to Zermatt or via the Gorner gorge (Walk 7).

WALK 13

The Gornergletscher and Monte Rosa Hütte

Start/finish	Rotenboden, 2815m on the Gornergrat railway
Distance	18km, 9km each way
Total ascent/descent	1000m in total (550m ascent/450m descent to the hut)
Grade	4
Time	8hr (4hr 15min to the hut and 3hr 45min back)
Max altitude	2905m, about 30min before reaching the hut
Refreshments	Monte Rosa Hütte, 2882m
Access	Rotenboden, on the Gornergrat railway
Note	GPX files for this route only show the general course of the glacier crossing as it will change from year to year.
Warning	This is a mountaineering route and should be undertaken only by walkers who are acclimatised, have high mountain experience and are comfortable crossing glaciers. Crampons are required for the glacier crossing.

The walk to the Monte Rosa Hütte is the hardest and perhaps finest walk that the Zermatt region offers. The futuristic-looking hut appears tiny on the vast mountainside of Monte Rosa but is in fact a substantial five-storey building. The route is more of a full mountaineering day than a walk, and you will certainly know you have done something if you complete the return trip in a day.

The route breaks down into three parts of broadly equal length: the descent from Rotenboden to the glacier, the crossing of the Gornergletscher and finally the passage across the rock mountainside vacated by the glacier, something of an epic crossing. This new route was developed in 2019, and the old route, which is likely to be shown on maps for some time, will be decommissioned from 2020.

The route crosses part of the Gornergletscher, which has some (currently small) crevasses. Crampons are necessary for this section and walking poles are very helpful. The final mountain crossing comprises a long section of moraines and rocks as well as some assisted sections. Marker poles sign the route on the glacier and the mountain section is well signed with painted marks.

It's a long trip. Time estimates vary from 3hr 20min upwards. We have given it a time of 4hr 15min out and 3hr 45min back, which is reasonable for a strong walker. With so much to see it could take a lot longer.

As it's a long and arduous route, it is preferable to enjoy a 5-star overnight stay in the hut and walk back the next day. Book in advance, though, as it's a popular place for both walkers and climbers.

The steep drops to the glacier below are several hundred metres high, a reflection of the melting in recent years.

From the station at Rotenboden head downhill and take the path left, signed 'Gornergrat and Monte Rosa Hütte'. This path crosses and then descends the steep hillside above the Gornergletscher. ◀ After 50min you will pass signs indicating that the new route continues straight ahead (The old route branched off to the right.) and in 10min you will come to the edge of the **Gornergletscher** at **2620m** (1hr).

Put crampons on and climb the glacier following the marker poles. The route will change from year to year, depending on the condition of the glacier, but essentially it climbs for about 2km to a level section of glacier and then turns right (south). Currently, there are a few small crevasses to get across or around; there are ways through with a bit of exploration. Once you have skirted the crevasses, the marked route heads downwards to the edge of the glacier and the moraine (2hr 30min).

The next hour and a half requires a high level of concentration, as the route crosses moraines and glaciated rocks as it contours round to the hut.

◀ Overall, the route is broadly level – but no two steps are the same. The constant change and undulating ground is quite tiring. Mountaineers would be used to this sort of ground, but walkers will find the going tough. The route is waymarked throughout with blue-and-white paint and some cairns at crucial spots. It's important to keep an eye on the waymarks, as it is easy to deviate from the track if not careful. A good eye for terrain will help keep you on the route. This being said, it is a great mountain journey set in immense grandeur, with Monte Rosa above, the Liskamm ahead and other Zermatt peaks, including the Matterhorn, constantly in view. Ensure you stop before you enjoy the view; every step requires concentration.

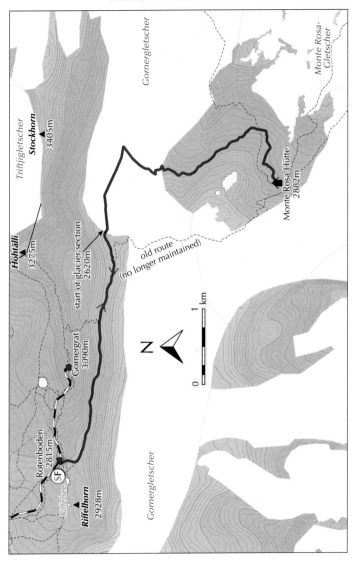

Cross rubble at the glacier edge, then continue over a crumbling moraine. Pass through intricate rocks and climb up what is almost a grassy section (the last on the route). Continue, climbing up rocky slabs and cross a second moraine. You will then make seemingly interminable ups and downs over the rocks. Some sections are protected by rope, a few others by metal steps. A few small streams drain from the glacier above. At one point a sloping ladder climbs across a gully; it looks awkward but has a good rope handrail. The terrain remains rocky and intricate. Cross a third moraine and after a further 10min you will reach the **Monte Rosa Hütte** (2882m, 1hr 45min from the glacier, 4hr 15min in total).

The current **Monte Rosa Hütte** was built in 2010 after the previous building had become unfit for purpose. The new hut, the most modern of its kind in the Alps, if not the world, benefits from the very latest technology, producing 90% of the energy it consumes. Accommodation for 120 people is in bunk bedrooms of 6, 7 and 8 people; it also has a winter room, restaurant and terrace. The original hut, Cabane Bétemps, was constructed in 1895 and accommodated 25 people. In 1939 the hut was extended and renamed the Monte Rosa Hütte. This building was demolished in 2011 and replaced by the modern hut we see today.

To return, simply reverse your ascent route. Keep an eye on the train times from Rotenboden back to Zermatt and take time to appreciate your achievement. You have definitely earned a large beer!

WALK 14
The mountain restaurants of Findeln

Start	Sunnegga, 2288m
Finish	Zermatt, 1620m
Distance	9km
Total ascent	80m
Total descent	750m
Grade	1–2
Time	2hr–2hr 30min
Max altitude	2288m
Refreshments	Sunnegga, Eggen, Findeln, Findeln Wildi, Ried
Access	Underground funicular to Sunnegga
Note	A steep woodland path descends from the restaurant Adler Hitta; the rest of the route is extremely easy walking.

Having the opportunity to explore the culinary delights of a number of restaurants when walking in the mountains might not seem very likely; however, this route is known as the Gourmetweg, so named as it takes in no less than six restaurants in the Findeln/Sunnegga area and a further two mountain restaurants on the return to Zermatt. There is also the promise of a fine balcony route overlooking Zermatt on a near-level path.

From the Sunnegga station walk out and descend left on a path and track to **Leisee**, a lake and recreation area just below. Walk through the gated recreation area and

The Restaurant Paradies (closed Wednesday and Thursday) is on the left; it has seating inside and outside on a terrace overlooking the valley, with the Matterhorn in the distance.

descend to reach a path-crossing and turn right. This leads directly into **Eggen**, a small collection of chalets and barns. ◄

Walk straight through Eggen and continue on a grassy contouring path, then turn sharp left onto a track and descend to reach the dispersed collection of chalets, barns and restaurants that make up **Findeln** (10–15min). Choose the restaurant, terrace and menu that most appeals!

Return up the hill the way you came, but when reaching the point where the grassy contouring path joined the track, turn left and walk down the track towards the enticing sunshades of the Adler Hitta restaurant at Findeln Wildi.

Now take the gently rising path behind the Adler, which skirts open hillside before entering woods and

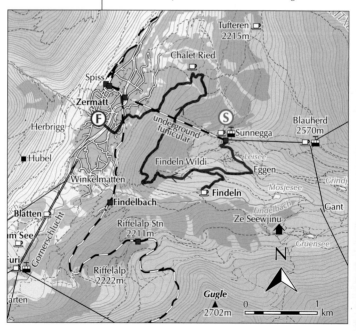

descending in a series of zigzags, occasionally quite steeply. Thirty minutes after leaving Findeln you will come to a signed path junction at 1985m; turn right.

The next thirty minutes of walking are a real delight, firstly for the **aerial views** down to Zermatt, and secondly because this must be one of the most level paths in the whole of the Mattertal. It's flat – really flat.

Enjoy the woodland walk, with occasional views or glimpses down to Zermatt, before reaching a junction of paths and tracks (1970m, 1hr from Findeln). To return directly to Zermatt take the path immediately to the left and descend, sometimes steeply through the woods (see the final section of Walk 20). For a continuation of the restaurant theme, turn left and walk down the track to reach another restaurant (1900m) in 15min. Continue on the track to reach a further restaurant at **Chalet Ried** (1805m). The track now leads directly down into the outskirts of **Zermatt**. Follow the road under the railway and over the river to the church in the centre of the resort.

The restaurant at Ried on the descent to Zermatt

WALK 15
Blauherd to Sunnegga
via Tufteren

Start	Blauherd, 2570m
Finish	Sunnegga, 2288m
Distance	4km
Total ascent	70
Total descent	350m
Grade	1–2
Time	1hr 30min
Max altitude	2570m
Refreshments	Blauherd, Tufteren and Sunnegga
Access	Sunnegga underground funicular from Zermatt, and Blauherd cable car from Sunnegga
Note	If walking this route in reverse, allow 2hr.

This is an easy path, never too steep, through the high, grassy, flower-strewn meadows between Blauherd and Tufteren. The path roughly follows the same route as a large grassy ski piste, always keeping to the north-east of the piste, through picturesque landscape. Several information boards along the route will help you identify the various flowers you pass by.

The path descends through rock-strewn meadows, covered in a multitude of flowers, and fine views towards the Zinalrothorn and Weisshorn can be seen ahead.

With your back to the Blauherd cable car station, a sign directs you left (north) on a level path. After 50 metres you will reach a further path junction. Turn left, signed to Tufteren. ◄

The path makes various broad zigzags from time to time, with the ski piste always to the left (west) of the path. Pass through a fenced area, and after 40min you will reach the path junction with the Europaweg (2260m). Turn left and walk down to **Tufteren** (2215m, 45min). ◄

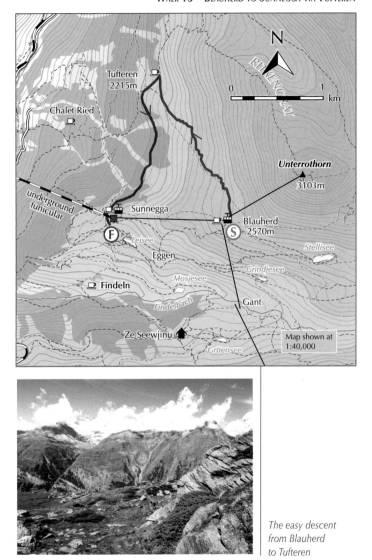

The easy descent
from Blauherd
to Tufteren

Tufteren is a small alp hamlet with a restaurant offering fine views from its large terrace. Paths from Tufteren lead to Sunnegga and down to Zermatt and to Täschalp, north on the Europaweg.

To return to Sunnegga, take the track heading south just above the restaurant, and follow this track as it slowly rises to **Sunnegga** (2288m, 1hr 30min).

WALK 16
The Five Lakes Walk in the Findeln valley

Start/finish	Sunnegga, 2288m
Distance	11km
Total ascent/descent	500m
Grade	2
Time	3hr 30min
Max altitude	Flue, 2618m
Refreshments	Flue, Ze Seewjinu (Seewjinen), Sunnegga
Access	Sunnegga underground funicular from Zermatt
Note	To shorten the route by 45min, take the cable car from Sunnegga to Blauherd, where a descending path leads straight to Stellisee.

This is a popular full day walking route visiting a series of five beautiful mountain lakes – four of them are natural and beautiful; the other, Mosjesee, is man-made and a bit of a disappointment. Every lake has a character of its own, and many provide superb photographic opportunities, particularly of mountain reflections on a clear, calm day. The route described here is a circuit from Sunnegga that includes a visit to Bergrestaurant Fluhalp, where refreshments (and beds) are available as well as an extensive sun terrace from which to admire the views towards the Matterhorn.

Leave Sunnegga station and turn left onto a rising path signed 'Stellisee 1hr'. Climb steadily, skirting the hillside

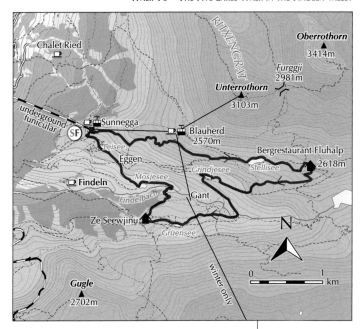

with the Findeln valley and village below, and the cable cars heading to and from Blauherd swinging lazily above. After passing just below the **Blauherd station**, the path eases, and a descending zigzag path can be seen to the right. Continue ahead, skirting a band of rock. The path from Blauherd joins from the left. Continue straight ahead to reach **Stellisee** (2537m). Bergrestaurant Fluhalp can be seen ahead (1hr).

> The views from **Stellisee** are stunning in all directions. The view considered the best, one providing reflections of the Matterhorn, can be seen from the far side, which is reached by a path that continues all around the lake. There are also views up the valley towards the Rimpfischhorn and the Findeln glacier.

Stellisee is well known for its reflections of the Matterhorn

From the far side of the lake climb a grassy bank to reach a track, then either walk up the track to the mountain hut, or take the signed path off to the left, which also leads directly in 20min to **Bergrestaurant Fluhalp** at Flue (2618m, 1hr 30min).

> **Bergrestaurant Fluhalp** has a fine terrace from which to admire the extensive views both down towards the Findeln valley and the Matterhorn and up the valley to the east.

From the restaurant terrace at Flue, facing south towards the moraine, take the descending track then turn immediately left, signed to Gant and Findeln, to enter an ablation valley with a high moraine to the left. ◄ Take the main path, signed to Grindjesee, down the valley to meet a track and turn left (20min from Flue). The track turns sharply right (with the moraine path joining at this point). Ignoring a steeply descending path to the left, continue on the track for 3–4min, then look for a path off to the right (the second or third paths are the easiest), dropping to join a small path running parallel to the track, through a meadow next to a stream. **Grindjesee** is just below (35min from Flue).

Another path rises to the crest of the moraine and can be followed to join a track lower down; however, this path is prone to erosion and is not recommended.

Grindjesee is a beautiful tranquil spot, surrounded on two sides by trees, with a grassy bank above from which there are abundant photography opportunities. The path around the lake then rejoins the track at a hairpin bend.

Return to the track and walk gently downhill. Continue straight ahead at a path crossing and ahead again when another track bends sharply right. Cross a stream, then turn right, signed to Grüensee. Pass under the cables of the Gant cable car, then a few minutes later take the small path up to the left to **Grüensee** (2300m, 1hr 15min from Flue).

Grüensee is in a particularly stunning location, enjoying classic views of the Matterhorn, but also, from left to right, the Ober Gabelhorn, Zinalrothorn and Weisshorn. It is a popular lake for picnics and even swimming on warm summer days.

Walk around the lake and at the western end take a path down to meet a track. Continue straight on, with Mountain Lodge Ze Seewjinu straight ahead (refreshments and accommodation). Now take a path on the right, still heading towards the building, that then turns right immediately before the restaurant building and descends through a pleasant, lightly wooded hillside, signed in the direction of Mosjesee. Cross the **Findelbach** stream at the bottom, then continue downhill on a track to the man-made **Mosjesee lake**.

At the western end of the lake a signpost directs you to a path rising steeply to the right towards Sunnegga. Climb this path, keeping straight ahead at a path crossing, (turning left leads to Eggen and Findeln) to reach **Leisee**, which nestles below a cliff, with Sunnegga above. ▶ To return to Sunnegga climb the track to reach a lower entrance to **Sunnegga station** and the train back to Zermatt.

The lakeside has been developed for tourists, with playgrounds and other facilities, and even an express funicular up to Sunnegga.

WALK 17
The Oberrothorn

Start/finish	Sunnegga, 2288m
Distance	16.5km
Total ascent/descent	1320m
Grade	3
Time	7hr
Max altitude	3414m on the summit of the Oberrothorn
Refreshments	Bergrestaurant Fluhalp (2618m) and the Unterrothorn station, Blauherd and Sunnegga
Access	Sunnegga underground funicular. Alternative starts are possible from Blauherd and Unterrothorn cable car stations, accessed from Sunnegga

The Oberrothorn is, by a very small margin, the highest walkers' peak in the valley and possibly one of the easier 3400m peaks in the whole of the Alps. Views from this height are outstanding in all directions. The summit pyramid involves a 440m ascent, presenting few problems for experienced walkers. This walk starts from Sunnegga and takes in Flue, with its welcoming *berghotel*, before climbing to a gentle col between the two Rothorns. At this point the character of the Oberrothorn is clear: rounded southern shoulders and a sheer northern face that plummets almost vertically having been eroded away by the Täsch glacier.

There are alternative start points for those who want more mechanical lift and less Bergrestaurant Fluhalp. Likewise, you can finish the walk at various points, but the following route ends at Sunnegga, from where there are several descent options.

Climb immediately above Sunnegga station, then under the **Blauherd cable car**. After 15min the path heads away to the right, with views across to the Gornergrat and a widening view up the Flue valley towards the Rimpfischhorn and Strahlhorn. Climb 300m on an easy silt path that has boards providing information on the lives of marmots

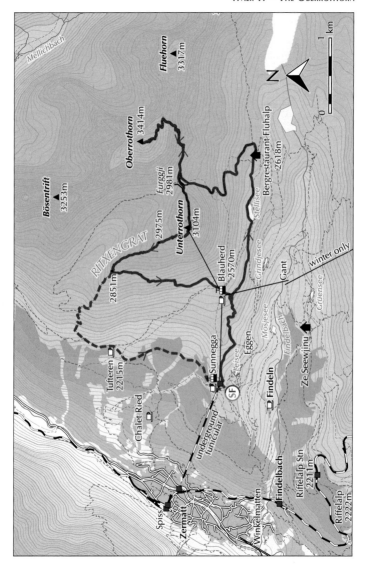

This part of the route has been named the Marmelweg or Marmot Way.

to enliven the route. ◄ Pass close under the cable car and continue to the beautiful lake of **Stellisee**, scene of many a photo showing the Matterhorn's reflection, before climbing to **Bergrestaurant Fluhalp**. Taking a path to the left avoids the track (2618m, 1hr 30min).

Behind the *berghotel*, various paths join at a sign after 3min. Take the left turn uphill. Cross a piste, then climb away from it, then meet it again and turn left uphill. Continue for some 400 metres before turning a corner to reach the path, climbing on grass. The track and path flirt all the way to the **Furggji col** at 2981m (2hr 30min).

From this side the mountain is a large, rounded hump; bulky and not immediately aesthetic.

The Oberrothorn path heads away to the right, climbing gently at first. ◄ The path heads east for 500 metres before starting to climb in zigzags. The path itself is almost entirely silt, with most of the mountainside being level stones. Numerous cut-through paths have been made over the years; these are best ignored. Pass an elegant cairn by a rocky outcrop, then walk through a short section of very thick (and possibly excessive) fixed rope. The path climbs into a shallow bowl and then views over the northern lip emerge, showing a very different side to the mountain, with cliffs that drop steeply down into the Täsch valley. The zigzags continue all the way to the top. Pass under a rocky outcrop to emerge on the summit of the **Oberrothorn** (3414m, 1hr 10min from Furggji, 3hr 40min from the start).

The immediate prospect on the summit of the **Oberrothorn** is the view to the Rimpfischhorn (4199m), a few kilometres to the east, but there are also 360° views across the Zermatt valley with most of the 4000m peaks visible. It's a fine viewpoint and well worth the climb.

Retrace your steps from the summit back down to the **Furggji col**, which takes 45min. Then climb the 120m to the building-festooned summit of the **Unterrothorn** (3104m, 1hr from the Oberrothorn).

There are various ways to descend from this point, but the main route, described here, heads directly down

The Rimpfischhorn and Strahlhorn from high on the Oberrothorn

the Ritxengrat ridge and returns to Sunnegga either via Tufteren or Blauherd. The path starts right under the front of the Unterrothorn cable car terminus. ▶ Descend into a rock-strewn landscape, the effect of retreating glaciers amplified by the effects of the ski industry. Pass a notch at **2975m** after descending for 20min and then continue along the Ritxengrat ridge, which is rocky with many twists and turns. Only at one point is it even slightly narrow. Drop down to reach a path junction at **2851m** in 35min and turn left towards the Blauherd station across boulder fields on a well-made path.

> It is possible to continue on the **ridge path** to Tufteren, but the ridge narrows and steepens and it is loose and exposed in several places, so only take this route if you are confident in such situations.

Building work currently taking place may affect the exact start in future years.

Cross by the **Blauherd station** and take an unsigned path (except for the label 'Marmelweg') right by the station. This descends sharply to join the path taken earlier in the day back to **Sunnegga** (30min from Blauherd and 3hr 20min from the Oberrothorn summit).

Other options
You could take the cable car down from Unterrothorn (although this was closed for renovation in 2019) or return to the Furggji col and reverse the ascent route; this has the added advantage of food at Bergrestaurant Fluhalp. Alternatively, descend north from Furggji into the long Tufterchumme valley, then return to Sunnegga via Tufteren (which also has food options).

WALK 18
Blauherd to Pfulwe and Täschalp

Start	Blauherd, 2571m
Finish	Täschalp, 2200m
Distance	13km
Total ascent	800m
Total descent	1180m
Grade	3–4
Time	5hr 15min
Max altitude	Pfulwe, 3314m
Refreshments	Bergrestaurant Fluhalp, Täschalp
Access	Funicular to Sunnegga then cable car to Blauherd. To descend from Täschalp see Walk 20 or take the late afternoon shuttlebus down into the valley

This traverse from the upper Findeln valley round to Täschalp will take you into wild backcountry and includes a small peak with spectacular views. It's a long walk, and an even longer descent if you walk all the way down to the

valley, but this can be shortened by taking transport from Täschalp. Take the first Sunnegga funicular and then the cable car to Blauherd to allow plenty of time.

The path over the Pfulwe col below the Spitxi Flue and Pfulwe peaks is graded 'alpine', a blue signed path. There are no difficulties on the ascent, or on the Pfulwe peak. The first half-hour of the descent is over steep, bouldery ground that faces north, holding snow in patches throughout the summer. The route then descends under rocks. Despite this, the path is very manageable, and for those who like remote wilderness, it is one of the best walks in the Mattertal.

From Blauherd, climb above the station and find signs to Stellisee lake. Descend gradually and pass the picturesque lake (25min). ◀ Follow the path then track above the lake to **Bergrestaurant Fluhalp** (2618m, 40min).

The views are best early in the day.

The path continues behind the hut, with signs indicating 1hr 40min to the col and 3hr 40min to Täschalp. Walk through the ablation valley, alongside the substantial (and steep) moraine left by the retreating Findeln glacier, then climb and pass through a higher valley with a small tarn (**2683m**). The path branches left up the hillside.

Pass a blue sign indicating you are now on the alpine stretch of the path (1hr 5min). ◀ Pass a grassy area and then keep to the good path as it climbs steadily, if steeply, to the **Pfulwe col**, where you will find a bench (3155m, 2hr 10min).

Behind you, the Matterhorn, standing alone, dominates the scene. To the right the Monte Rosa and Liskamm rise above the Gornergrat.

The climb up Pfulwe takes around an hour for the round trip and includes 160m of ascent and descent. It is well worth it, unless the weather is poor, as it is a fine viewpoint over the whole region, especially towards the remote Rimpfischhorn and Strahlhorn. The ascent is very lightly indicated by white marks, upturned stones and cairns, but the route is clear to see. Follow the trail and as you approach the summit, you will pass a larger cairn. The summit of **Pfulwe** (3314m) is a little way to the right – but take care as there are some large drop-offs to the east. ◀ Reverse the climb to return to Pfulwe col (3hr 10min).

The 360° views encompass virtually the whole Zermatt valley.

The Oberrothorn seen from the summit of Pfulwe with the Weisshorn and Zinlarothorn in the background

Descend directly north from the col on the path. ▶ The path drops through boulders, snow and possibly icy terrain, passing another bench after 15min.

Here the path drops down to the right under a rock outcrop. It is steep and there is some limited protection in a couple of places (a pole to hold onto and some metal steps) but you will soon pass this stretch, and 30min after leaving the col there are no further difficulties.

The route continues to descend steadily on a moraine, gradually steepening. Pass a closed path to the Täschhütte and continue to drop down. After descending for an hour, you will reach a point where the path becomes a track where you ford a stream. Continue along the track until you reach **Täschalp** (2200m, 5hr 10min). Refreshments are available at the **Europaweghütte** 100 metres further on.

As it faces north there is likely to be some snow all through the summer; if you find snow reaching up to the col and are not equipped to deal with it, you would be better to return to Flue.

WALKING IN ZERMATT AND SAAS-FEE

The beautiful upper Täsch valley

Options from Täschalp

There are several possible ways to return to Zermatt:

Wait for the afternoon shuttlebus to Täsch and then take the train back to Zermatt. The shuttle currently runs at 1700 but check with the tourist information office in Täsch before setting out.

Take one of the descent options to Täsch (see Walks 19 and 20). Both are steep; the direct path takes 1hr 30min and the longer route takes around 2hr to descend.

Take the Europaweg path (see Walk 20) to Tufteren (1hr 45min) and Zermatt (3hr). This route will be shared by Tour of Monte Rosa and Chamonix to Zermatt trekkers.

WALK 19
Täsch to Täschalp and the Täschhütte

Start	Täsch railway station, 1438m
Finish	Täschalp, 2200m
Distance	12km
Total ascent	1260m
Total descent	480m
Grade	2
Time	5hr
Max altitude	2700m
Refreshments	Europaweghütte at Täschalp, Täschhütte
Access	Railway at Täsch, shuttlebus to Täschalp
Note	If you want to begin the walk from Täschalp and save a two-hour 800m ascent, a shuttlebus service runs between Täsch tourist information centre and Täschalp twice daily (0930 and 1700) between July and mid October. Check at the tourist information centre to confirm times before departing.

This is a fine day out that can be shortened or lengthened in a number of ways to suit most walking parties. Although the route from Täsch to Täschalp involves 800m of ascent, the path climbs at a steady gradient through woods, which will tend to be shaded and cool until mid morning. The climb from Täschalp to the Täschhütte is a popular high mountain outing on a straightforward route, following a track all the way, with extensive views that improve as you gain height. The Täschhütte, which offers accommodation for walkers and climbers, is an ideal place to have lunch before heading back down to Täschalp.

From the railway station at Täsch cross the main road, and with the tourist information centre on your right walk straight up the village road. At the top turn right, then turn almost immediately left to climb with the stream on your right. At the top of this road cross the bridge and then

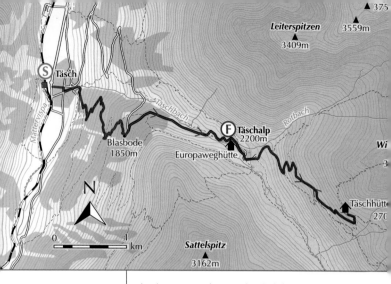

take the rising path immediately left, signed to Täschalp. The route climbs past the back of some chalets in big zigzags. After 10min cross the road, and cross again 3min later and continue to climb.

After just under 1hr join a track and turn left then immediately right onto another steep path to emerge at a small clearing with two wooden crosses; drinking water is available here (**Blasbode**, 1850m). Maintaining direction continue on a rising path to reach a road at a hairpin bend (1hr 20min). Turn right and follow the road as it continues to climb. ◄ Continue up the road to reach **Täschalp** and the **Europaweghütte** (2200m, 2hr 30min).

The climb from here to the Täschhütte takes 1hr 30min. Walk up the road through the scattered village and turn right onto a track in front of a long, low farm building. The track then curves left, with the **Rotbach stream** and valley ahead. The track then swings right to climb the hillside, meeting a path junction at a hairpin bend after 25min.

Continue up the track, passing a signed path off to the left to Weingarten. The track continues to rise at a steady gradient with the Täsch Hut now clearly visible up ahead. Resist any temptation to climb more directly to the hut as you draw near (the path is steep and loose).

After 300 metres a signed path to the right provides an option to join the Europaweg path. This is a short steep climb that soon turns left to Täschalp or right to Tufteren and Sunnegga (signed 2hr 30min).

Instead, keep on the track, swinging left and up to arrive at the **Täschhütte** (2700m, 4hr). ▸

An optional path runs below the track, but this is narrow and poorly maintained. It has considerable exposure as it traverses the steep hillside and is not recommended.

> The views from the **Täschhütte** are extensive; to the west the Weisshorn and Zinalrothorn and their tumbling glaciers dominate, while to the south-east lie the Oberrothorn and the deep verdant Täsch valley far below. The hut is used by climbers tackling the neighbouring peaks of the Täschhorn and Alphubel, and on a sunny day the terrace is often crowded with climbers and walkers enjoying the stunning scenery.

> To return to Täschalp, simply reverse the ascent route, following the track all the way (5hr).

Options from Täschalp
- Take the afternoon shuttlebus back to Täsch.
- Return to Täsch on the path through the woods (1hr 30min).
- Follow the Europaweg (see Walk 20) to Tufteren or Sunnegga and continue down to Zermatt (3hr).

The Täschhütte on a sunny day is busy with walkers and climbers

WALK 20
Täschalp to Zermatt

Start	Täschalp, 2200m
Finish	Zermatt, 1620m
Alternative finish	Sunnegga, 2288m
Distance	9.5km
Total ascent	250m
Total descent	830m
Grade	2
Time	3hr
Max altitude	2340m on the trail above Tufteren
Refreshments	Täschalp Restaurant and Lodge, Tufteren
Access	To reach Täschalp take the train from Zermatt to Täsch, then a shuttlebus to Täschalp, which runs twice daily. Alternatively, you can walk up from Täsch: a climb of 800m that takes 2hr (see Walk 19)
Warning	A section under the Bösentrift mountain is particularly prone to rockfall and there are warning signs and shelters on this section.

The route from Täschalp to Zermatt is a fantastic balcony route with superb views of the Weisshorn followed by the mighty Matterhorn on the final section of the Europaweg, which means you will share the path with walkers doing the Chamonix–Zermatt Walkers' Haute Route and the tours of the Monte Rosa or the Matterhorn. Between Täschalp and Tufteren the path gains and loses 250m, before the descent into Zermatt. Waymarking is for the Europaweg, Swiss Route 27.

This route could also be used as a finish for the Täschhütte walk (Walk 19) or the Pfulwe route from Blauherd (Walk 18).

From the Täschalp car park, just above the Täschalp Restaurant and Lodge, drop down to cross the Täschbach stream and then climb onto the level route. The Weisshorn is seen directly across the Mattertal from Täschalp, while views back towards the Täschhorn give a closer perspective of this challenging mountain.

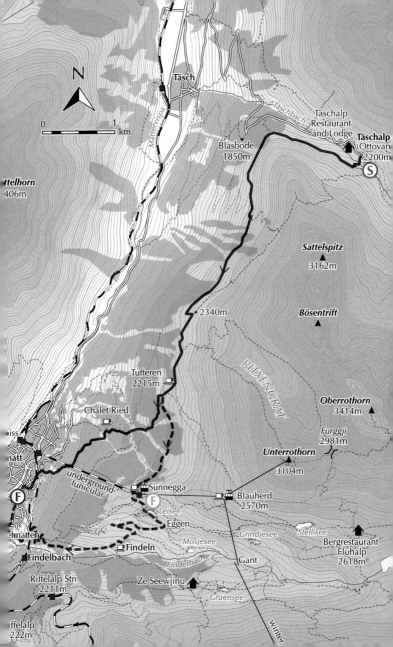

N

0   1
⊢———┼———┤ km

Täsch

Mattervispa

Täschbach

Täschalp
Restaurant
and Lodge

Blasbode
1850m

Täschalp
(Ottovan)
2200m
S

ttelhorn
406m

Sattelspitz
3162m

2340m

Bösentrift ▲

RIIXENGRAT

Tufteren
2215m

Oberrothorn
3414m ▲

Chalet Ried

Furggji
2981m

iss

Unterrothorn
3104m ▲

natt

F

underground
funicular

Sunnegga
F

Blauherd
2570m

Leisee

Eggen

Grindjesee

Stellisee

lmatten

Mosjesee

Findeln

Bergrestaurant
Fluhalp
2618m ▲

Findelbach

Findelbach

Gant

Riffelalp Stn
2211m

Ze Seewjinu ▲

Gruensee

ffelalp
222m

winter

Continue along the broadly level path. After 20min you will pass a path turn to Täsch. The path continues ahead just above the treeline and descends gradually before approaching the section that is exposed to rockfall. The path meets a track at a hairpin bend and then climbs, not steeply but it feels tiresome on a hot afternoon, to reach a high point (**2340m**) with superb views to the south towards the Matterhorn. The path then steadily drops towards the hamlet of **Tufteren** with its restaurant (2215m, 2hr).

From Tufteren descend steeply, still following Route 27. After flirting with a mountain bike track (take care, they move quicker than a walker can think!) continue down to meet a track and turn left. After 30 metres, where the track heads right and a path joins from the left, you will reach the continuation of the path descending past a wooden barrier. This drops in steady loops through woods, eventually coming out above Zermatt where you are presented with a choice of paths to the station, the church or Winkelmatten. For the church descend on wooden steps followed by stone steps with a handrail before emerging near where the Gornergrat railway line passes overhead. Turn left on the road under the railway line and follow this road to the bridge in the centre of **Zermatt** and then on to the church.

Descent from Tufteren via Sunnegga

To reach the Sunnegga underground funicular station, continue along the almost level track from Tufteren (30min). At **Sunnegga** either take the funicular down to Zermatt or continue down to **Findeln**, where there are several restaurants and cafés, and walk down to **Zermatt**, a descent of 670m that takes 1hr 15min (see Walk 6).

GRÄCHEN, RANDA AND THE LOWER MATTERTAL

Preparing to tackle the suspension bridge on the Europaweg (Walk 21)

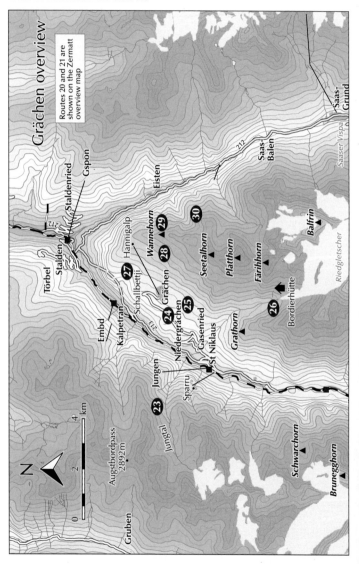

Grächen overview

Routes 20 and 21 are shown on the Zermatt overview map

Grächen is a relaxed resort, ideal for families and those who prefer a more intimate base

Grächen lies on a shelf 500m above St Niklaus and is a good base for exploring the lower part of the Mattertal. The village can be reached by road from St Niklaus either by car or by taking the twice-hourly bus from the station, which takes 20 minutes to climb up to this small, attractive resort.

The village has all the facilities you would expect and is especially suitable for family holidays; however, its position on the main Tour of Monte Rosa trekking route and its proximity to the Chamonix–Zermatt/Europaweg route (see below) mean it is also well used by trekkers. It is also a start/finish point for the well-known Grächen–Saas-Fee Höhenweg (see Walk 30).

Grächen itself has several hotels, restaurants, cafés, shops and a tourist office covering Grächen and St Niklaus. Plenty of apartment accommodation is available through the tourist office, and in addition a Grächen Goldcard is available either to purchase or free of charge if participating-partner accommodation is booked through the tourist office for more than four days. The card includes one free Gornergrat railway trip, one free Jungen trip, unlimited Hannigalp trips and a variety of other local offers. Car parking is spread around the central square and the Hannigalp cable car; most of the rest of the village is car free.

The area is a prize-winning family ski resort, and the gondola and other facilities are available in summer as well. The facilities in the village are capped by the Hannigalp gondola, which rises to 2100m, giving access to higher walks in summer as well as the many ski pistes during the winter ski season.

Grächen's western outlook means it gets the sun in the afternoon and evening, allowing some walks to be tackled on cooler mornings. The outlook from the village takes in the Weisshorn and surrounding peaks to the south, the Jungen area directly across the deep Mattertal and views across the Rhône valley to the Bernese Alps in the north.

The walking options from Grächen have several characteristics. At around village height, 1600–1650m, a series of fairly level paths, some alongside waterways from the Bärgji area high at the northern end above Stalden through to Gasenried in the south, provide ample walking for those not wanting serious ascent or descent. Higher up, the Hannigalp cable car provides several walking opportunities both up and down, while the routes towards Gasenried and the nearby Riedgletscher allow easy access to the glacier, more so than many other alpine areas.

Grächen is also a good base for exploring the lower Mattertal around St Niklaus and Randa. Buses down to St Niklaus meet trains along the valley, so most start points for other walking routes can be reached within 45min from the village.

In short, walks from Grächen can either be very easy or very hard.

Two points of warning: according to the map, the Seetal area looks like a good high-walking destination; however, the closure of the high-level path from Hannigalp, due to serious and dangerous rockfall, and the fact that there is nothing interesting other than ski pistes when you get there mean this area is best avoided. The apparent path to a col leading to the Saastal should be left well alone. Many older maps show paths in this area but check the 1:25,000 Grächen area map first for the best information.

Next, the well-known Europaweg (Swiss Route 27) starts in Grächen and continues to Zermatt. This route originally took a high line on the eastern side of the Mischabel wall separating the Saastal and Mattertal. Following dangerous rockfall this route has now been closed. A new path takes a lower route to Herbiggen, then on up to the Europahut, Täschalp and Zermatt.

OTHER VALLEY BASES

St Niklaus is a busy town in the valley, more a working town than a destination for visitors, although the old town area is attractive. There are several restaurants and a couple of hotels, as well as shops and cafés, but it is more suitable for an overnight stop than a longer stay.

Randa is a small village higher up the railway line to Zermatt. With an information centre, a hotel, a single shop with limited opening hours, a couple of restaurants and several apartments, facilities are somewhat limited. Walking opportunities directly from Randa centre around the Charles Kuonen Hängebrücke and the Europaweg, and tend to be very steep!

Other villages between St Niklaus and Grächen, including Gasenried, Niedergrächen, Rittinen and Bodmen, have limited apartment accommodation, but they would require transport (or bus trips) to the start of most routes so would only suit those with a car who particularly want to be outside the main village. **Gasenried** is a 40min walk from Grächen and benefits from its own direct bus service to St Niklaus. It has a small village store and a restaurant, and B&B accommodation at the Berghaus Alpenrösli.

There are no special discounts on Grächen lifts, but the Half-Price Card is accepted on the Hannigalp cable car. There are only two lifts for walkers in the area:

The **Hannigalp** gondola lift, which rises from Grächen to Hannigalp at 2200m, runs from 0830 to 1730 between June and September. It costs CHF15 one way before discounts.

Jungen is serviced by a small lift, with priority given to residents. It's unmanned and runs between St Niklaus, where the ticket office is located (250 metres from the station), and Jungen. The half-price Swiss card doesn't cover this lift, although one

The Ried glacier

The restaurant at Hohtschugge (Walk 25)

trip is included with the Grächen Goldcard. Operating times are between 0630 and 1940, and the cost of a one-way trip is CHF12.

HUTS AND RESTAURANTS

As well as restaurants in Grächen, there are restaurants in Gasenried, Zum See, Hannigalp, Bärgji and Hohtschugge. Above St Niklaus, Jungen has a restaurant that can be accessed by the small lift (or a 2–3hr steep uphill walk). St Niklaus has hotels and restaurants.

The **Bordierhütte** at 2886m is the start point for climbs on the 4035m Dirruhorn and the 3795m Balfrin, among other peaks. It is nearly five hours' walk from Grächen, including a glacier crossing, so most walkers would need an overnight stay. The hut sleeps 40 in dormitory accommodation. Tel +41 279 561 909, www. bordierhuette.ch (online booking is preferred), email: info@bordierhuette. ch.

WALK 21

The Europahütte and Hängebrücke to Täschalp

Start	Randa, 1407m
Finish	Täschalp, 2200m
Alternative finish	Randa, 1407m
Distance	13km (alternative 7km)
Total ascent	1480m (alternative 840m)
Total descent	680m (alternative 840m)
Grade	3
Time	6hr; alternative 4hr 15min
Max altitude	2265m at the Europahütte
Refreshments	Randa, the Europahütte and Täschalp
Access	By train to Randa. Use the twice-daily shuttlebus from Täschalp to Täsch at the end of the route
Note	Check locally to ensure there are no closures on the Europaweg to Täschalp. Crossing the bridge in windy or thundery conditions is inadvisable.

The new Charles Kuonen Hängebrücke (suspension bridge) is the longest of its type in the world and one of the wonders of the valley. However, this walk includes two other attractions: the Europahütte and the Europaweg itself, which is crafted into the mountainside under the Dom and Täsch mountains, providing a route high above the valley. As you progress south, the Zermatt peaks and Matterhorn come into closer view.

The route involves a lot of ascent and a long and at times slightly exposed traverse that has plenty of protection in the form of cables, occasional footways, metal steps and even a short tunnel. The bridge itself is very solid, but even so it spans a gap of 500m, suspended almost 80m above the gorge of the Dorfbach stream, and those crossing it will need a head for heights. Saying that, pretty much everyone seems to make it across; there is room to pass and the bridge seems very solid.

There is an opportunity to split the route into two, spending the night at the Europahütte. In this case the first day would be 2hr 30min and the second 3hr 30min. A descent to Randa is also given for walkers who just want to experience the bridge.

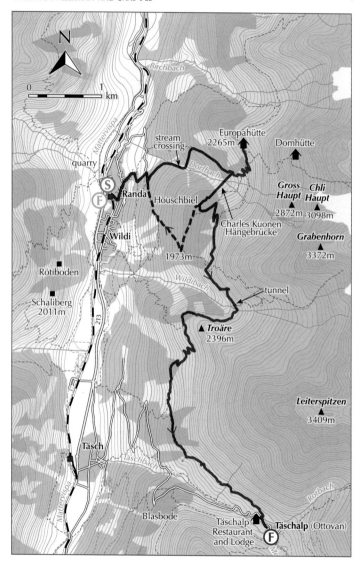

From Randa station turn right along the road and then left into the quiet hamlet of Randa, which has many older buildings. Continue straight on as you leave the village on a good path across pastures and you will arrive at the **Dorfbach stream crossing** (1534m, 30min).

Cross the stream and take the upper path, now signed to the bridge and hut. The path climbs more steeply in zigzags through forest. You will then reach a path junction (1890m, 1hr 15min). ▶

Climb steadily for the next 40min to arrive at the **suspension bridge** (2016m, 2hr).

Looking back, you will see the remains of the vast landslide that came down in 1991. Thankfully, it took no lives but it left a vast fan of debris across the valley floor.

THE CHARLES KUONEN HÄNGEBRÜCKE

The suspension bridge is just under 500m in length

This engineering masterpiece was installed in 2017 across the dangerous Dorfbach gully, replacing an earlier 250m bridge that was swept away in 2013. The longest pedestrian suspension bridge in the world, it is evidence of the commitment of the local authorities and people to this high-level route. Hanging 80m above the gorge, it is impressive in every respect, and for a bridge of this length it is remarkably solid to walk across. In spite of this, it will be a challenge for those who don't have a head for heights; in which case it would be best to return to Randa by your ascent route.

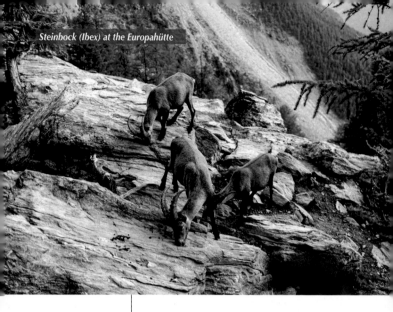

Steinbock (Ibex) at the Europahütte

If staying overnight, call ahead to book a place; the hut is a popular stop on the Chamonix–Zermatt and Monte Rosa trails.

Continue for a final 25min on steep zigzags to reach the **Europahütte** (2265m, 2hr 30min). ◄ If you want to miss the hut out and continue to Täschalp, you will save 45min and around 150m of up and down.

The descent from the hut to the bridge takes 20min. Put walking poles away, and anything else you are holding, and strike out confidently across the 494m-long bridge, which will take you about 10min at a slow but steady pace.

Descent to Randa

A direct descent to Randa takes just under 1hr 45min. After crossing the bridge keep right, as Täschalp is signed left at **Höüschbiel** (2053m). Turn sharp right, 10min after crossing the bridge, at the **1973m** path junction and head down through woods, keeping straight ahead until reaching **Randa**. Turn left down the main street and continue down to the station.

The continuation to Täschalp takes 3hr 30min from the Europahütte. Keep left at **Höüschbiel**, following Swiss

Route 27 Europaweg signs. After crossing a level, open mountainside, with good views across the valley to the Weisshorn and south to Zermatt, continue to contour at close to 2200m, entering the deep bowl of the Wildikin, which is aided by cables and a **short tunnel** – with a light switch! The high traverse continues with the Dom and Täschhorn mountains above. Pass concrete avalanche and stonefall protection, then climb briefly over a small ridge and head steadily down to **Täschalp** (2200m, 6hr), also known (and labelled on maps) as Ottovan.

It is possible to walk back down to Täsch (1hr–1hr 30min), but it has been a long day, the descents are steep and it may be better to restore the inner walker at the Täschalp Restaurant and Lodge before taking the shuttle-bus down to Täsch (currently at 1700 but check before setting off).

WALK 22
Schaliberg alp

Start/finish	Randa, 1408m
Distance	8.5km
Total ascent/descent	620m
Grade	2–3
Time	3hr 30min
Max altitude	2011m at Schaliberg
Refreshments	None on the route; restaurants in Randa
Access	Randa is reached on the main valley railway line

The Dom and Täschhorn dominate the middle section of the Mattertal but getting a good view of them is a challenge; however, this can be achieved in the following half-day walk to Schaliberg alp high above Randa. The Dom at 4545m is the highest mountain located entirely in Switzerland; the Täschhorn is slightly lower at 4491m. Both are difficult mountains for climbers. Schaliberg allows you to glimpse their impressive higher slopes and secrets.

As well as offering exceptional views, Schaliberg, perched 600m above the valley on a rocky buttress, is an example of how tough life was, and in some cases still is, for Switzerland's farmers. Little husbandry takes place now, as the call of the tourist industry is clearly felt by the younger generation, but you can readily imagine the tough life of those who worked the land here.

It is a place of tranquillity and beauty, a place to watch the changing perspective across the valley as the sun swings south then west, a place to look across at and wonder how the high paths on the east wall were made and how they will survive. And it is a place to watch the flowers and birds gradually take back control of this lonely alp. You are unlikely to be disturbed, except perhaps by climbers heading for the 2930m Weisshornhütte, some 2hr 40min higher.

From Randa station turn right and head south. Keep heading south towards **Wildi** and in the village turn right and cross (in sequence) the railway line, the main road to Täsch and the **Mattervispa river** (10min).

Turn left after crossing the river and continue south. The path climbs a little then drops back down to the river. Cross a footbridge over the river and immediately recross it on a bridge carrying an access track. There are two ways to climb to Schaliberg, both of which turn off from this path; our route is the second turn. Pass the first turn and continue onto a **golf course**, the Matterhorn Golf Club, which will be on your left. ◄ At a house and equipment store, you will find the second turn to Schaliberg (1430m, 35min).

The manicured course sits in stark contrast with the severe and rocky hill above that you will shortly climb.

Turn right on the small path and climb steeply. As you climb you are joined by paths from the right but keep on climbing. ◄ Ahead is the gorge of the **Schalibach**, carrying the outflow from the Hohlichtgletscher. The Zinalrothorn sits proudly above the glacier. Climb away from the gorge and pass barns tucked under a cliff. The path continues to climb steeply on open hillside with good views. As you approach the Schaliberg alp, a path

The village of Täsch is below, the former open-air car park now flat meadows along the riverside. The station apart, Täsch is now a quiet village.

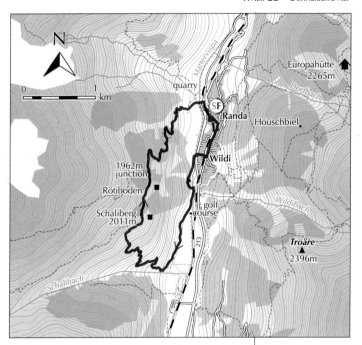

heads off left to the Weisshornhütte; it would take 2hr 40min to reach the hut, so this is clearly one for climbers – and walkers with considerable energy reserves. The alp comes into sight and soon you reach **Schaliberg** (2011m, 2hr 15min).

> After the bustle of the valley and the heat of the climb, **Schaliberg alp** is a tranquil place, where old farm buildings, now little used, hint at the hardships endured by farmers not so long ago in order to look after their animals. Across the valley and high above, the upper reaches of the Dom and Täschhorn are clear to see, as are the peaks above Täsch, while the Breithorn dominates the southern end of the valley above Zermatt.

129

Elegant barns on the descent into Randa

Rötiboden is an open pasture with just two farm buildings.

Pass along a high walkway, protected by wooden railings, and continue to a second alp, **Rötiboden**, a 15min level walk further on. ◄ Immediately after Rötiboden there is a second turn up to the Weisshornhütte. Continue on the level path for a further 5min and you will reach the **1962m** path junction, where a path heads steeply down (2hr 30min).

Take this path down, which crosses grassy pastures initially but then enters a wood after 3min. Pass close around the top of a chasm to the right and continue down. It is a steep path but well made for (and doubtless by) the farmers who managed the alp. As you approach the bottom, you are likely to hear the clanking of large machinery at the quarry just north of Randa. Pass through a picnic area, a series of attractive old barns and signs for a *spielplatz* (playground). Continue down past the **quarry** and across the river and the railway. Turn right under the road and right again to arrive back at **Randa station** (1408m, 3hr 30min).

WALK 23

Jungen, Sparru and the Jungtal

Start/finish	Jungen cable car top station, 1980m
Distance	11km (5km if walking directly to the Jungtal from Jungen)
Total ascent/descent	760m
Grade	3 (Grade 2 if the direct route from Jungen to the Jungtal is used)
Time	4–5hr (2–3hr for direct route)
Max altitude	2357m in the Jungtal
Refreshments	Jungen restaurant
Access	Cable car from St Niklaus
Note	The cable car takes just four people at a time, and at peak times it operates at a maximum frequency of every 15–20min. Residents of the alp hamlets are given priority, so you may have to wait. Allow plenty of time.
Warning	The route from the point where the Jungbach torrent is crossed to Sparru and beyond to the Jungtal is often on very exposed ground, making this route a Grade 3. Some rope and cable protection is in place, but at other times the path may feel a little too narrow to be ideal on the exposed hillside!

This superb, challenging walk visits two alp hamlets, Jungen and Sparru, to reach a high point in the remote Jungtal, with views up to the Rothorn (3278m) and Furggwanghorn (3162m), separated by the Jungpass at the head of the valley. Views across the valley towards Grächen and to the Ried glacier are superb. The return to Jungen is on an easy, well-graded path that comes as a reward at the end of the walk. If you prefer something less challenging, simply walk from Jungen up to the Jungtal on the path described as the descent route, following signs for the Jungtal.

Perched high above St Niklaus, Jungen is a traditional alp village made up of a collection of old barns and chalets, a tiny chapel and a picturesque natural lake with a small restaurant just above. Sparru is even smaller: a dispersed alp hamlet on a neighbouring hillside, with access from St Niklaus via a steep zigzagging path (not described) or from Jungen by the path described. Both villages enjoy superb views and a wonderful sense of peace and remoteness from the trappings of modern life. However, with easy access by cable car, Jungen is often busy on sunny days.

From the cable car at Jungen, walk to the left and down to the cluster of chalets that forms the main part of the village and turn left signed for St Niklaus. Pass between ancient chalets and barns, then follow the path down in a series of lazy zigzags through woods. Just after passing a second small shrine, look carefully for a small unsigned path to the right (1.2km, 1680m, 30–40min)

The path drops to the Jungbach as it tumbles through its spectacular gorge. Cross the **Jungbach** on the concrete bridge. The path on the other side is initially almost level, but then climbs steeply across an exposed, mainly wooded, hillside with cables and ropes for reassurance, and with great views down into the gorge and across the

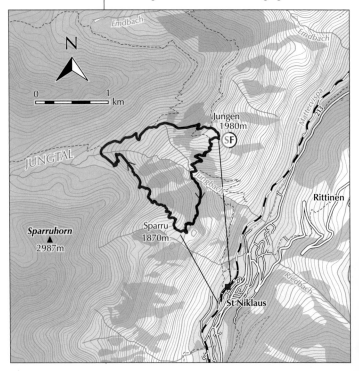

Mattertal to Grächen and Gasenried. Pass a turning to the left signed to St Niklaus (this is the only path up from the valley), then ignoring all other turns to the left, continue climbing in a series of tight zigzags to reach **Sparru** (1870m, 1hr 30min). ▶

From Sparru the path to the Jungtal is signed all the way. First take the path straight up across a meadow towards a higher group of chalets, then turn right, climbing steadily, then swing left, climbing steeply almost straight up the grassy hillside. After about 150m of ascent the path weaves its way through a rocky section, then continues steeply in zigzags through the lightly wooded

Take care: the path is steep and covered in small fir cones, pine needles and other debris so can be quite loose and slippery.

The challenging route to Sparru

133

hillside. At 2070m the path divides. Take the right-hand fork, which curves steeply around to the right of a large area of rock. (The path shown on the map takes the left-hand fork, but this is closed as it is dangerously exposed and has now been replaced by the right-hand path.)

Continue zigzagging up the hill, then pass into a bay in the hillside and climb steeply out on an exposed path with cables for reassurance. The gradient suddenly eases as you skirt around the hillside now opposite Jungen, which can be seen far below, the ground carpeted with bilberries, alpenrose, juniper and wildflowers (2260m, 3hr). Drop down 30m to join a small water channel and follow it for about 500 metres, then begin to climb the final 100m of ascent, into a side valley to avoid a cliff, to emerge at the **Jungtal** (2387m, 3hr 30min).

> The **Jungtal** is a long, wide and remote valley, with a small alp chalet and long barn for livestock, seen a short way off. Take a little time to walk up and enjoy the full extent of the valley and the mountains forming the backdrop to the view.

The restaurant by Jungen's small cable car and lake

From the Jungtal sign, turn right, cross the **Jungbach** and take the path to Jungen. The path makes a long, easy descent to reach a path junction at 2200m, then continues easily down, following an old stone wall, before swinging right to descend through woods to **Jungen** (1980m, 5hr). ▸ On sunny days there may be a sizeable queue for the cable car down to St Niklaus, so be prepared to wait. The 800m walk down is hard on tired knees and not to be recommended.

The restaurant just above the cable car is excellent.

WALK 24
A tour of the villages – Grächen and Gasenried

Start/finish	Grächen, 1610m
Distance	6.5km
Total ascent/descent	230m
Grade	1
Time	2hr 30min–3hr
Max altitude	1725m
Refreshments	Grächen, Gasenried
Note	Niedergrächen is on the bus route to Grächen, providing a possible way to shorten the route or avoid the final 130m climb to Grächen.

Most of the walks described from Grächen tend to explore the paths above the village; however, the lower slopes have a network of paths that reveal a softer, rural landscape as they thread their way between the villages and hamlets. This circular walk follows the Bineri water channel to Gasenried and includes an excursion to climb the Grächbiel, an isolated knoll with views across to Grächen, the Riedgletscher and the snow-capped peaks of the Mischabel mountains beyond.

From the church and tourist information centre walk east up a steep pathway towards the sports centre, then turn right in 30 metres and take the path branching right,

135

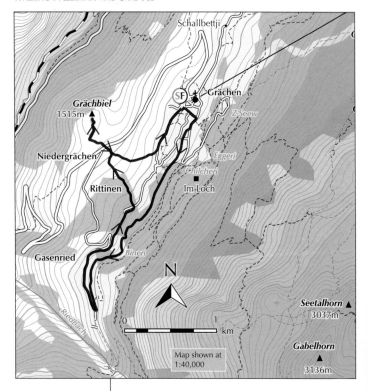

which crosses a small area of meadow next to the end of the Bineri water channel. Follow this between chalets and then enter the woods. Follow the Bineri all the way through the woods, crossing a huge gully (Ritigrabe), with signs warning of mudslides, after 20–25min. Emerging from the wood, continue following the Bineri across a meadow above Gasenried. The path eventually meets a track at a hairpin bend. Descend to the road at the far southern end of **Gasenried**. Turn right and walk into the village (1659m, 40min).

Gasenried is a much larger village than is immediately apparent from the buildings along the main road through the village, with scattered houses stretching down the hillside for at least 100m. There is a restaurant and a small general store, and the village also benefits from a bus service directly to St Niklaus.

Having explored the village a little, continue on the road in the direction of Grächen. Pass the fire station (with WC sign), then take the path opposite (to the right), which skirts the hillside, back through the woods. Cross the Ritigrabe gully once again and continue on the upper broad path until it meets a track with a small picnic area just to the left (1630m, 15–20min from Gasenried).

Turn left then immediately right by the picnic area to drop down through the woods, keeping straight ahead at a path crossing. Ignore a path to the left 100 metres further on, then pass between chalets to emerge and turn

Immaculate chalets and gardens in Niedergrächen

WALKING IN ZERMATT AND SAAS-FEE

The isolated hill of Grächbiel can be seen ahead across the road.

left onto a broader path that leads down to a small white chapel next to the road in **Niedergrächen**. ◀

> **Grächbiel** is an odd little hill, covered with rough grass and small rocky outcrops. Its northern side is steep and precipitous, but walking on the southern side is easy, and the views to Grächen are well worth the excursion.

To walk up to Grächbiel and back take a small tarmac road immediately to the right of the bus stop opposite the chapel. (Another track 10 metres away is signed to Grächbiel, but currently this route is not well maintained and should be avoided.) Walk down past chalets, then fork slightly left at Chalet Guxu, keeping to the right of a grassy area as you climb towards a chalet and small old wooden barn. Turn right and climb across the hillside, passing three flagpoles on your right to arrive after 500 metres at a large cross on the summit of **Grächbiel** (1515m, 10min). There are fine views across to Grächen and Gasenried and two well-sited benches on which to sit and admire the view. To return to Niedergrächen simply retrace your route back to the main road.

Cross the road and, once more, take the path signed to Grächen behind the chapel. Keep left on the main path as it climbs steeply and steadily to reach the outskirts of Grächen near the Hannigalp Hotel. Turn left and walk back into **Grächen** (1.2km from Niedergrächen, 30–40min). Alternatively, you can catch the bus to avoid that last steep climb!

WALK 25
Grächen leat paths – the Chilcheri and Eggeri

Start/finish	Grächen, 1610m
Distance	11.5km
Total ascent/descent	340m
Grade	1–2
Time	3hr–3hr 30min
Max altitude	1810m
Refreshments	Hohtschugge, Bärg (Bärgji) and Grächen
Note	The paths by the leats (water channels) are almost level; however, tree roots and rocks make this level walk unsuitable for pushchairs, particularly on the Chilcheri. This route can be shortened easily by taking a descending path above Z'Seew.

Walking beside running water channels in the shade of wooded hillsides is an ideal choice for a hot summer day. The only sounds you hear are those of the movement of the water and the occasional scuffle of the squirrels in the trees, with the mild scent of fresh pine permeating the air. This route explores most of the length of the two upper water channels – the Chilcheri and the Eggeri, with a return via the restaurants in and around Bärg (Bärgji on signposts).

The route can easily be shortened by returning to Grächen at a path junction and picnic area at 1784m, just above Z'Seew.

From the main square take the path east rising between restaurants and chalets towards the sports centre. Turn right then immediately left onto the path, with the sports centre now on your left. Climb for 2–3min to find a path junction and take a right turn, signed for the Chilcheri. Walk through the wood and up through a playground area and cross part way over a small meadow then fork left towards a chalet (**Im Loch**) and pass below the chalet to enter woods. The path is clearly signed and is always

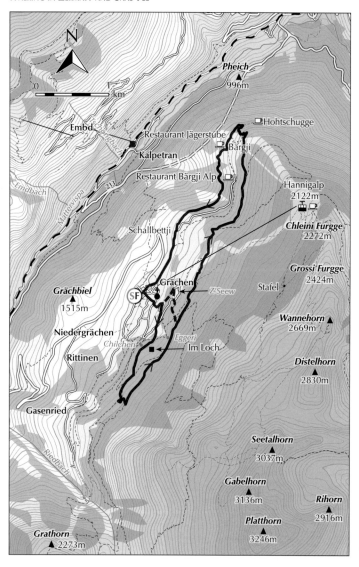

next to the water channel. After 30min you will arrive at a point where the Chilcheri is carried across the dry streambed of the Ritigrat in a long flexible black water pipe.

Drop below the pipe into the streambed and climb steeply up the other side to a path junction (1770m) and turn sharp left. ▶ Cross back over the stream bed and climb very steeply on a good path, then turn right and climb steeply again to reach the **Eggeri** (1810m, 50min). Turn left and begin to follow the Eggeri on its long gentle descent.

The Eggeri path is slightly broader and the woodland slightly sparser, allowing for better views to the west

For a longer walk, the Chilcheri continues for a while beyond this point to well above Gasenried.

A waterwheel on the Chilcheri leat

141

across the valley. Pass tiny waterwheels set above a series of large hollowed out logs, and after 30–40min you will reach a picnic area and path junction (1784m). To make a shorter circular walk, turning left leads directly to the Z'Seew lake.

Continue ahead with the distant rumble of the Hannigalp cable car now apparent. Cross a piste with the **cable car line** above, then continue ahead still with the Eggeri for company. ◀ Continue ahead, ignoring more path crossings, until eventually the weary Eggeri (now probably dry) finishes as the path passes under a ski lift and crosses a piste to reach a path junction. Turn left and descend steeply in a series of zigzags through woods to a track at 1630m (2hr–2hr 15min).

In summer the water starts to dry up shortly after this point.

> The restaurant **Hohtschugge**, 100 metres to the right, enjoys superb views to the north towards the Bernese Oberland, with Stalden seen far below.

Turn left to meet a larger track at a hairpin bend. The two restaurants in **Bärg/ Bärgji** are found to the left. Walk past the first restaurant, then find a small descending path crossing a meadow and turn left to continue downhill. This is a lovely path that threads its way across the hillside, undulating through woods. Keep left at a path junction to eventually emerge at a small collection of chalets at Schallbettji, 1630m, at the far northern end of Grächen. Walk down the road for 1km to reach the centre of **Grächen**.

WALK 26
The Ried glacier and the Grathorn

Start/finish	Grächen, 1610m
Distance	15km or 19.5km
Total ascent/descent	780m or 1120m
Grade	2 or 2–3
Time	4hr 30min or 6hr 45min
Max altitude	2238m above Alpja or 2460m above Grathorn
Refreshments	Grächen and Gasenried (off route but easily accessible)
Warning	Do not continue above Grathorn; the path is closed and is dangerous.

Grächen is fortunate in its proximity to the Ried glacier, which brings water through the various watercourses. The glacier is also close enough to the village for you to visit inside a walking day. This makes for a long day, but a good viewpoint can be reached within 2–3hr, with options to climb higher if time allows.

The walk includes an optional climb to the Grathorn, a great viewpoint north and into the Mattertal and through to Zermatt. But **do not go further** as this is the dangerous closed section of the Europaweg.

It is also possible to climb to the Bordierhütte, which is nearly 5hr from Grächen and for most walkers will require an overnight stay. At the crossing point the glacier is dry and clear, but crampons as well as glacier experience are strongly recommended.

From the church in the centre of Grächen climb towards the sports centre, then take the steep path to the right of the sports centre and turn right to join the trail of the Chilcheri waterway. This continues, past Gasenried, for 4km. Climb, following signs to Alpja, to the end of the Eggeri waterway (1827m, 1hr 15min).

Many **routes to Gasenried** are possible, with four water leats, the paths between them, as well as the

143

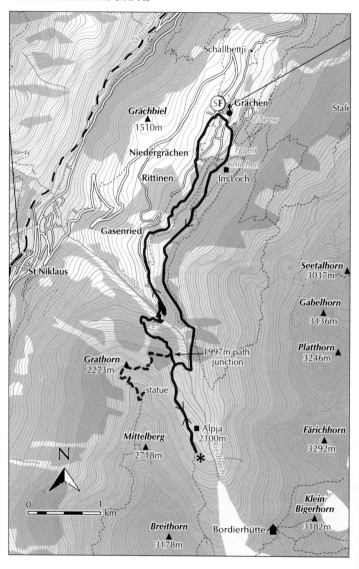

main walkway, so select your preferred route. The Chilcheri, however, does provide a good start point for the rest of the walk.

Climb steadily on the good path, crossing a stream (don't get distracted by an apparent route climbing the stream; the correct route is straight across). In 10min pass a left turn to Seetal and continue ahead towards the Riedbach stream, which is clearly heard, and towards the moraines of the glacier, which come into sight soon.

Climb steadily and closer to the **Riedbach**. It becomes apparent from the level of noise that it carries most of the drainage from the glacier. Cross a bridge with a view directly to the glacier. Keep right after the bridge and climb the moraine, meeting another path 10min on from the bridge.

Turn left and wander through the increasing idyllic ablation valley (a valley created by a glacier between its moraine and valley walls) that develops between the vertical walls of the Grathorn to the right and the ever higher

The Riedgletscher from the high point on the route

moraine wall to the left. You will reach the remote summer farm of **Alpja** (2100m, 2hr).

The moraine is close to vertical. The view down to a remnant of the lower glacier and the icefall lies above.

To get a view of the glacier continue through the valley with the glacier and mountains ahead. The glacier tumbles down, and the path can be seen high above, climbing through the scree alongside the moraine. For a good view of the glacier, approach carefully where the path meets the moraine wall at 2238m. ◂

This route stops at this point to allow time to take in the Grathorn. But if you want to see more of the **Ried glacier**, climb another 500m to over 2700m where the path crosses the glacier (2hr 30min round trip).

Retrace your steps to Alpja (20min) and continue down past the path you arrived on, dropping down to a path junction at **1997m**. At this point there is a choice: either continue the descent to Gasenried and onwards to Grächen (4hr 30min) or take in the Grathorn viewpoint.

Optional visit to the Grathorn and Europaweg statue

The path wends its way through the forest and onto the hillsides above, where alpenrose vies with juniper for attention.

At the 1997m path junction, turn left on a smaller path that climbs steeply for the next 50m but then steadies. ◂ The climb zigzags and 50min after the turn you will arrive at the **Grathorn** (2273m), the northern outpost of the Mischabel mountains and a surprisingly flat area. Far-reaching views stretch north towards the Mattertal and right through to Zermatt.

Climb 150m higher to find the **Europaweg statue** perched on a promontory looking towards the views in the south. This is the point to stop. From here onwards the Europaweg is closed – so **go no further**! Return to the Grathorn and then drop back down to the **1997m** path junction (2hr 15min round trip).

To continue the route to Grächen, from the 1997m sign descend a good if steep path. As you approach a track, you may meet obstacles designed to deter walkers, coming in the other direction, from taking the closed

Europaweg. Join a track and climb to the Schalbettu chapel and continue on the road into Gasenried (1659m, 3hr 40min, or 6hr 10min if you climbed the Grathorn).

To return to Grächen continue through Gasenried and after a bend in the road take a path that climbs a little through pastures but then becomes fairly level. Cross the probably dry Ritigrabe gully (signs warn of mudslides) and continue on a track that becomes a tarmac walkway into **Grächen** (1620m, 4hr 30min or 6hr 45min).

The Europaweg monument looks over the Grathorn

WALK 27

Hannigalp to Grächen via Hohtschugge and Bärgji

Start	Hannigalp, 2122m
Finish	Grächen, 1620m
Distance	6.5km
Total ascent	100m
Total descent	600m
Grade	1–2
Time	2hr
Max altitude	Hannigalp, 2212m
Refreshments	At Hannigalp, Hohtschugge and Bärgji, then Grächen
Access	Cable car to Hannigalp

This is a delightful route down from Hannigalp, with the added attraction of several restaurants at the halfway point after you have completed most of the descent. Different in character from the higher mountain walks in this guide, the route goes down through woodland abounding in wildlife for around an hour, with views of the Rhône valley and the Bernese mountains glimpsed though the trees, before turning and contouring past farms to emerge in Grächen. There are many ways from Hannigalp back to Grächen at the 1600–1650m contour level, but the small woodland path recommended is quiet and interesting.

From Hannigalp, take the broad grassy track dropping down to the north, signed to Hohtschugge, that descends a small ski piste. After 10min turn right at **2050m** by a small ski tow. The path enters woods and contours east for 400 metres before starting a steep drop. This is the steepest drop on the route, after which there is nothing steep, although there is plenty of downhill to do.

The woods are teeming with wildlife. Take time to stop and listen to the chattering squirrels high in the trees.

Descend on the well-made path, losing height all the time. ◀ Look out for a right turn on a smaller path at 1853m (30min). This descends in zigzags, passes the end of the Eggeri waterway path, where you keep right,

and then drops in more zigzags to a wide track. The **Hohtschugge restaurant** is 100m to the right, with wide open views north over the Rhône valley and the Bernese Alps (1619m, 1hr).

Return to the track, which soon joins another track at a hairpin bend. Keep left and climb to a collection of chalets, barns and two restaurants that make up the hamlet of **Bärgji** (1hr 10min).

Two routes head to Grächen from here. The higher route climbs towards the Eggeri waterway, which could be used (see Walk 25), providing access to various other paths into Grächen.

The lower path is a better option here. Drop down to the right alongside a barn and turn left on a track, which almost immediately becomes a path. It descends past a house but then contours, alternately climbing and descending, through a series of gates and the farm at Gobe. It continues, crossing woods and pastures in an elegant thread before emerging by a group of houses at the very northern extreme of Grächen. The path then becomes a small road, climbs a short way and continues

Hannigalp cablecar and restaurant

149

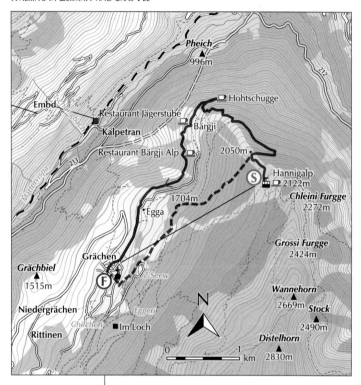

down through the hamlet of **Egga**, emerging in **Grächen** by the bottom Hannigalp lift. Continue down to and along the main street into the town centre (1620m, 2hr).

Alternative route to Grächen

This descent to Grächen provides a quicker alternative to the main route described, avoiding both the steep and stony direct descent track from Hannigalp, as well as the somewhat dispiriting route beneath the cable car line. Turn left not right at the **2050m** junction 10min below Hannigalp and descend on a beautiful path through woods, before joining the Eggeri waterway at **1704m**

(40min). Turn left and after a further 5min turn right keeping to the right of a piste and the cable car line, then left under the cable car onto a track dropping down to the Z'Seew lake (1hr) and then continue down into **Grächen** (1hr 15min).

WALK 28
Grächen to Hannigalp via Stafel

Start	Grächen, 1620m
Finish	Hannigalp, 2122m
Distance	5km
Total ascent	600m
Total descent	100m
Grade	2–3
Time	2hr 15min
Max altitude	2204m at Stafel
Refreshments	Grächen and Hannigalp
Access	Return to Grächen by cable car; other options are available

This route explores the attractive woods above Grächen, which are full of wildlife, and offers extensive views across the western side of the Mattertal. It's a fairly easy and short half-day walk, with one steep, rocky stretch to exercise the lungs; the route could be extended, however, into a 3–4hr walk if desired. You will reach the cable car and restaurant at Hannigalp in good time for lunch.

At the end of the route you can take the cable car back down to Grächen or walk down via several possible routes, including Walk 27, which passes a number of restaurants below Hannigalp and has tremendous views north towards the Bernese mountains and west to the Augstbordpass and the Jungtal high above St Niklaus.

From the church in the centre of Grächen take the narrow street climbing above the central square and walk

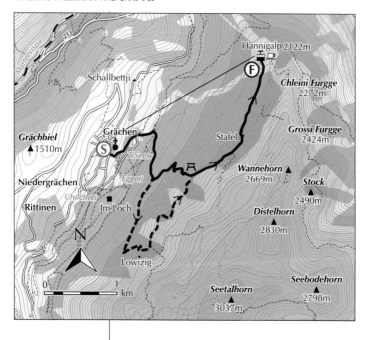

up to the sports centre. Take the well-signed path that climbs past and then above the centre and then steepens to reach the **Z'Seew lake** (1720m, 20min).

Climb the steep track and after 5min take the second of two right turns, signed to Stafel. The path, which climbs steadily through woods, is described as a *naturweg* and *waldweg*.

After 20min take a smaller path turning left (45min). This is well signed and waymarked. It climbs in intricate turns through an increasingly rocky hillside in the woods. ◀ Watch for a sharp right turn in the route. (Another path – not waymarked – continues straight ahead; if the waymarks stop, you have gone too far. Return until you find the red-and-white marks again.) The route becomes steeper and rockier, weaving through ever larger rocks. Just when it seems the path will steepen

Forest flowers cover the ground and squirrels chatter in the trees.

forever, the gradient eases and you arrive at a **picnic area** where a path joins from the right.

Z'Seew lake above Grächen

The wood becomes sparser with more views across the valley to the Jungtal. Cross a boulder field on a well-built pathway. The path angle is gentler here, and soon after you will reach the **Stafel** clearing (2204m, 1hr 55min).

Take the broad track leading down to **Hannigalp** (2212m, 2hr 15min).

Options from Hannigalp
- Descend by cable car to Grächen.
- Take either the steep track or the path under the cable car to Grächen. Both take about 1hr but are steep and have little to recommend them.
- Continue on Walk 27, which returns to Grächen in 2hr, passing a series of restaurants.

Longer route to Stafel and Hannigalp via Lowizig
Instead of making the left turn direct to Stafel after 45min, continue on the *naturweg* path and continue to **Lowizig**. Turn left at 2207m after 50min and cross the hillside just above tree level, passing several rocky bands before coming out by the **picnic area** just before Stafel. This adds 45min to the route.

153

WALK 29

Ascent of the Wannehorn

Start/finish	Hannigalp, 2122m
Distance	6.5km
Total ascent/descent	570m
Grade	3
Time	3hr 30min–4hr
Max altitude	2669m
Refreshments	Hannigalp
Access	Hannigalp cable car from Grächen
Note	The exact route from Hannigalp to Chleini Furgge can change when ski infrastructure and grazing areas are defined. If in doubt, follow yellow signage to Chleini Furgge for the first part of the route.
Warning	The ridge path (Gemsweg) is more challenging, as it involves some exposure and a fair amount of clambering over rocks, although you won't need to use your hands. It also occasionally passes close to cliff-edge drop-offs on one side. This route is suitable for fit families, provided the children are confident on mountain paths.

This excellent route to a mountain top provides variety, some excitement and fantastic views in every direction. The Wannehorn (2669m) can be reached via a high mountain path that picks its way on or near a ridge line or via less exposed paths and tracks, if preferred; you can combine the two on a round trip. The ridge route is recommended as an ascent route, with the descent at least partly on a track.

Much of the hillside has been shaped for ski pistes and access tracks, but the route described here avoids these as far as possible, and the ridge path in particular takes you far from the scarred hillsides and into a world where ibex and chamois can often be seen.

From the exit of the Hannigalp cable car station turn right and walk 30 metres to a path sign and continue ahead on a rising track towards the Wannehorn (signed

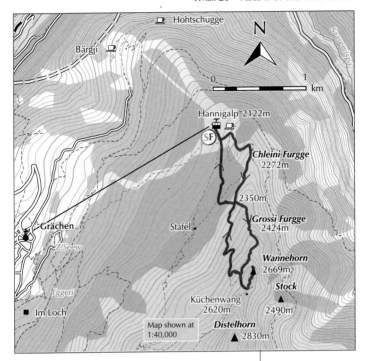

'Wannihoru'), with a playground to the right. At the next junction turn left up a short, steep section of track. (A path leads ahead up through woodland; this is an optional ascent path that will be used later for the descent.) At the top of the track turn right on a path just in front of a chairlift building and climb steeply up the side of a grassy piste. The path swings right, then left to reach the beautiful grassy saddle of **Chleini Furgge**, 2272m, with views across to the northern slopes of the Saastal and north to the Bernese Oberland (2272m, 20min).

The rocky ridge towards the Wannehorn can now be clearly seen ahead. The track turns right and continues, then forks left at the next track junction, still climbing. A path signed to the left is an option for reaching Grossi

Furgge, or you can continue on the track for a further 5–10min to where another path crosses the track, with a sign pointing left to Grossi Furgge (2350m, 40min). Take the path to the left and climb steeply for 10min through bilberry, juniper and alpenrose slopes to reach **Grossi Furgge** (2424m, 50min).

> **Grossi Furgge** enjoys tremendous views across and down into the Saastal. It's a broad grassy area and a fine point to reach for a shorter walk before returning to Hannigalp.

Turn right (south) and begin the climb. The narrow path climbs steeply, threading through boulders and rocks and gaining height quickly. After 30min the route swings left to enter a magical cleft and a grassy saddle from which the summit looms clearly ahead. ◄ The gradient eases, and a short climb brings you to a large boulder field. The route is clearly marked with numerous red-and-white paint splashes as you skirt the hillside, climbing gradually. Eventually, a path emerges from the boulders to reach a junction with a track at 2590m. Turn left onto the track and climb steeply for 5min to **Küchenwang** ('Chuchiwang' on the sign), 2620m, then

This is a quiet corner where ibex and chamois can often be seen.

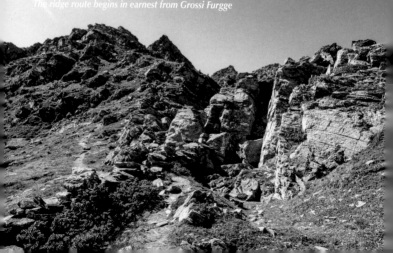
The ridge route begins in earnest from Grossi Furgge

follow the path now heading north to reach the summit of the **Wannehorn** (2669m, 2hr from Hannigalp). The secondary summit, which has a large iron cross and a summit record book, is just ahead across boulders, 14m below the true summit.

> On a clear day you can enjoy panoramic views from the summit of the **Wannehorn**: to the south-west the icy Weisshorn (4506m), the Bishorn (4153m) to the right and the Brunegghorn (4164m) in front. To the north the Bernese Oberland dominates the distant view, with Visp seen far below. To the east the Saastal, with Saas-Balen surrounded by green pastures, lies over 1000m below, while the Weissmies (4017m) dominates the skyline. The snow-covered peaks just seen to the south-east are the peaks of the Mischabel range above Saas-Fee.

To descend, retrace the path and track down to **Küchenwang**, then take the path straight ahead, passing below and to the left of a small wooden chalet/shelter. The path zigzags down to join a track. Turn right onto the track and descend through two hairpin bends to reach a path junction at 2350m 20min later. This is the path junction reached earlier, with **Grossi Furgge** signed to the right.

Take the path left, descending at first steeply through alpenrose and bilberry, cross straight over a track and descend again now less steeply through lightly wooded hillside to reach a confusion of paths and tracks, with the Hannigalp cable car station seen ahead. Walk down the track, with the playground now below and to the left, to reach **Hannigalp** (2122m, 3hr 30min).

> A short walk up the hill in a northerly direction from the Hannigalp cable car station brings you to a modern **chapel** at a prominent viewpoint. The chapel is deliberately very simple, with the views of the mountains providing all the decoration and inspiration needed.

To return to Grächen, either take the cable car down in under 10min or use one of the descent routes described in Walk 27.

WALK 30
The Grächen to Saas-Fee Höhenweg

Start	Hannigalp, 2122m
Alternative start	Grächen, 1620m
Finish	Saas-Fee, 1800m
Distance	17km
Total ascent	700m
Total descent	1010m
Grade	3
Time	6hr 45min
Max altitude	2384m
Refreshments	Hannigalp and Saas-Fee only; none en route
Access	By cable car to Hannigalp

The Grächen to Saas-Fee Höhenweg (sometimes referred to as the Balfrin Höhenweg) is undoubtedly one of the highlights of the region. The pathway, first constructed in 1954, works its way across the hillsides between the two resort villages at a middle mountain height. The path is good, with ample cable protection where needed, but it is probably best avoided by those who struggle to cope with heights – the drops are impressive.

The Saastal lies far below, usually over 1000m down; first Saas-Balen and then Saas-Grund are seen as miniatures. Across the valley the Fletschhorn, Lagginhorn and Weissmies creep gradually closer through the day. The trail passes under the Wannehorn, the Balfrin and later the Nadelhorn and Lenzspitze, which stand high above to the west.

Despite the views, the trail demands full concentration as it weaves through mountain bays and cliffs. No special equipment is needed but check with the tourist offices (or visit their websites) to make sure the trail is open – hard snow and rockfalls would change the character of the route. We have suggested a slightly longer time than the 6–6hr 30min given on signs. These are walking times only, so the trip will take a full day.

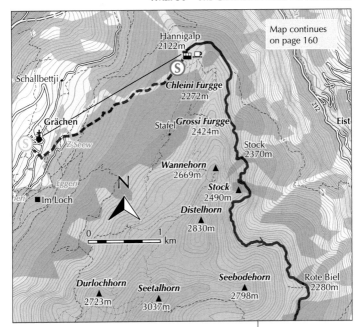

Map continues on page 160

Alternative start from Grächen

If you are purist and want to walk from Grächen, climb on the steep path from the centre of the village, past the sports centre and **Z'Seew lake**, and continue steeply up a broad track to **Hannigalp**. This climbs 500m and takes nearly 1hr 30min, making the whole route some 8hr in total.

From the Hannigalp cable car station and restaurant, take the broad track climbing across pastures. After 5min you will pass a beautiful, modern chapel in a stunning location with glass windows looking out over the mountains. Climb steadily to about 2300m, and as the path turns south it also narrows. It contours at this level with some ups and downs until Rote Biel. You will arrive at the first of the high, narrow paths and cable sections that are a

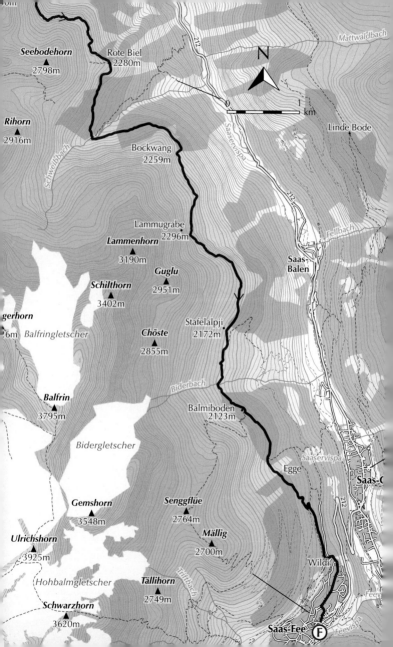

Seebodehorn
2798m

Rote Biel
2280m

Rihorn
2916m

Bockwang
2259m

Lammugrabe
2296m

Lammenhorn
3190m

Guglu
2951m

Schilthorn
3402m

gerhorn

Balfringletscher

Chōste
2855m

Stafelalpji
2172m

Balfrin
3795m

Bidergletscher

Balmiboden
2123m

Egge

Gemshorn
3548m

Senggflüe
2764m

Ulrichshorn
3925m

Mällig
2700m

Hohbalmgletscher

Tällihorn
2749m

Wildi

Schwarzhorn
3620m

Saas-Fee Ⓕ

Linde Bode

Saaservispa

Saas-
Balen

Fellbach

Biderbach

Saaservispa

Saas-C

212

N

0 ——— 1 km

feature of the route. Pass under the Grossi Furgge and Wannehorn before coming to the first natural break point at **Stock** (1hr 30min).

The next part of the route traverses a vast mountain bay (geologically a truncated side valley) under the Distelhorn and Seebodehorn, with the Grossus Gufer gully between them bringing sections prone to stonefall. ▶ The high-level path traverses enormous coast-like bays and a short tunnel for the next hour until you reach **Rote Biel** (2280m, 2hr 30min).

This is probably the most severe section of the route.

Continue and descend into the next 'bay', which carries the **Schweibbach** stream. The going here is more straightforward. Pass the stream crossing (2100m, 3hr). It is possible to descend to the valley here, midway between Saas-Balen and Eisten. Climb steadily from the stream (another 30min) before crossing through a section of steep cliffs with near-vertical drops to the valley almost 1000m below. The paths are good and protection is provided when needed. Here, you are passing under the 3190m Lammenhorn, an outlier peak of the 3795m Balfrin. Continue, to arrive at the lonely signpost announcing you have reached **Bockwang** (2259m, 4hr).

A sign gives an early warning of stonefall, encouraging you to move quickly through this area.

From Bockwang, climb steadily over open mountainside. ▶ You will then enter a large area of rockfall that seems reasonably stable, but you should cross quickly. Turn a ridge and cross another stonefall area, and you will

Much of the route is on a good, but exposed path

come to a sign at **Lammugrabe** (2296m, 4hr 45min). This is the name of the stone chute you have just crossed.

The route continues through rocks in a wonderful passage suddenly more akin to Tolkein's Shire, with flowers and wildlife for the first time in some hours, before the mountainside opens again and you arrive at **Stafelalpji** (2172m, 5hr 10min). Here, a descent to Bidermatten and Saas-Grund is possible. Continue on the *höhenweg*, passing through tunnels under the murky **Biderbach** stream that drains the glacier above, and you will arrive at **Balmiboden** (2123m, 5hr 40min) where a path joins from Mällig (see Walk 33).

Continue on a gentle downwards incline through woods. The path, rocky for so long, now softens, with tree roots to trip the tired walker. Swiss Route 13 turns downhill at Senggboden but continue on the signed *höhenweg*, keeping left at the next path junction and descend past the woodland cottage of **Egge** to a path junction at 1904m (6hr 20min).

Head left on a track for 100 metres and follow it round a hairpin bend. Continue on this track for 25min to arrive in the **Wildi** 'suburb'. Continue into the village and follow signs for the tourist office and bus station in **Saas-Fee** (1800m, 6hr 45min).

The vantage points and views along the höhenweg are exceptional

SAAS-FEE AND
THE SAASTAL

The Stausee Mattmark (Walk 49)

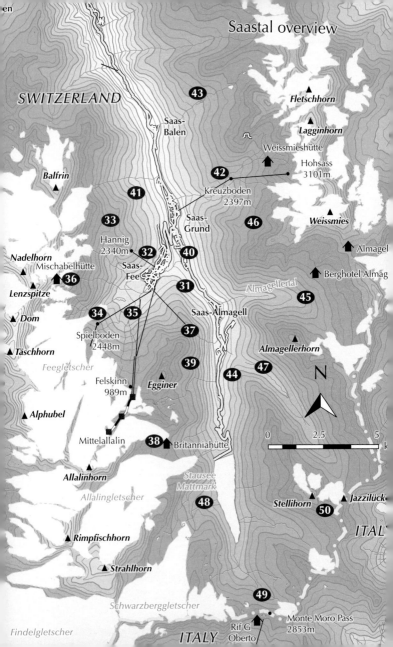

en

Saastal overview

SWITZERLAND

Fletschhorn ▲

Saas-
Balen

43

Lagginhorn ▲

Weissmieshütte

Balfrin
▲

41

42

Hohsass
3101m

Kreuzboden
2397m

33

Saas-
Grund

46

Weissmies ▲

Nadelhorn ▲
Mischabelhütte

Hannig
2340m

32

40

Almagel

Lenzspitze ▲

36

Saas-
Fee

31

Berghotel Almag

Almagellertal

▲ **Dom**

34

35

Saas-Almagell

45

▲ **Täschhorn**

Spielboden
2448m

37

Feegletscher

39

Almagellerhorn ▲

Felskinn
989m

Egginer ▲

44

47

N

▲ **Alphubel**

Mittelallalin

38 ▲ Britanniahütte

0   2.5   5

k

Allalinhorn ▲

Stausee
Mattmark

Allalingletscher

48

Stellihorn ▲

Jazzilück ▲

50

▲ **Rimpfischhorn**

ITAL

▲ **Strahlhorn**

49

Schwarzberggletscher

Monte Moro Pass
2853m

Findelgletscher

ITALY

Rif G
Oberto

Saas-Fee and its neighbouring villages have been well-known mountain resorts for over a century. Although it is best known as a ski resort, the lifts, transport and path network make Saas-Fee a superb summer walking destination with walks at all levels of difficulty.

The Sass valley contrasts markedly with Zermatt, its bigger, noisier cousin just a valley away. Where Zermatt is all energy, Saas-Fee is quieter, less international, smaller, friendlier maybe, but it offers just as many walking opportunities for the visitor.

The region covered in this guide is based in the upper Saas valley. From Visp, the lower valley heads up to Stalden where it forks; the western branch leads to St Niklaus, Randa, Täsch and ultimately Zermatt. The eastern branch rises past small villages and hamlets through a narrow section of the valley containing the Saaservispa river before broadening out near Saas-Balen, the first of the Saas villages. Shortly thereafter lies Saas-Grund, the largest village in the main valley. Onward roads climb to Saas-Fee, which sits in a hanging valley to the west, and Saas-Almagell,

Saas-Fee lies in a hanging valley, cradled by the 4000m peaks of the Mischabel range

with the remote Stausee Mattmark the buses' final stop at the head of the valley.

The villages are linked by an excellent bus network, so there is a wide choice of places to stay. Each village has a tourist office and shops.

Saas-Fee, 1800m, is the largest centre in the Saastal. It sits on the edge of its mountain bowl, a huge hanging valley surrounded by an array of peaks – the Allalinhorn, Alphubel, Täschhorn, Dom, Lenzspitze and Nadelhorn to name only the 4000ers. With several lifts, circular walking routes and a full range of accommodation and other facilities in the village, Saas-Fee alone provides options for well over a week's walking. The only downside is the need to drop down into the valley to access routes starting from Saas-Grund and Saas-Almagell. The resort is car free, and all vehicles need to be left in the car park at the roadhead.

Saas-Grund, 1560m, sits at the foot of the 250m rise to Saas-Fee. Gondolas take you up onto the Weissmies range, to Kreuzboden and Hohsaas. The resort faces the Mischabel giants, giving it broader views, and with a good range of accommodation, among other facilities, as well as being the transport hub for the region, it is a strong alternative base to Saas-Fee. Routes from Saas-Grund climb towards Saas-Fee

and run up and down the valley, making extensive use of the Kreuzboden gondola.

Saas-Almagell, 1670m, lies further up the valley. It has more limited facilities and accommodation (but ample) and access to many of the best walks in the region. Routes from Saas-Almagell run into the high and wild Almagellertal and the nearby Fürggtalli, which is capped by the Antronapass. The Mattmark is used as a base for remoter walks up to the Italian border at the Monte Moro Pass.

Saas-Balen, 1483m, has fewer facilities (although it currently boasts an Indian restaurant) and fewer walking opportunities directly from the village, so it is a less obvious walking base than the other villages.

As a visitor staying in the Saas valley, you are issued with a Citizens' Pass providing free access to all buses above Saas-Balen as well as all the lifts. This is a major boon, and over a week's holiday it will save you a significant amount of money if you make good use of the transport and lift systems; it may be the deciding factor in which resort to visit.

Postbuses link all the villages in an integrated network. Saas-Fee is a 10-minute ride from Saas-Grund, with

The berghaus at Almagelleralp

buses running twice hourly. The bus ride from Grund to Almagell takes 10 minutes, running at least hourly, and the trip to Mattmark takes less than 30 minutes.

The main lifts are as follows:

From Saas-Grund the **Kreuzboden–Hohsaas gondola** takes walkers high up on the eastern slopes of the valley to reach the Weissmieshütte and *höhenweg* routes to the north and the south.

From Saas-Almagell the small **Furggstalden chairlift** rises to 1901m for walkers exploring the Furggtälli. Another chairlift takes walkers to and from Heidbodme at 2346m, where there is a viewpoint and access to routes towards the Antronapass.

From Saas-Fee the **Hannig gondola** rises to 2245m, providing access to tours above the valley and the summit of Mällig.

There is also a gondola from **Saas-Fee to Plattjen**. Both the Hannig and Plattjen lifts occasionally close, but never at the same time.

The main cable car system from Saas-Fee runs to an interchange with access to Spielboden and Längflue and to **Felskinn**.

MOUNTAIN HUTS AND RESTAURANTS

A range of huts provide destinations for day walks and overnight stays.

Mischabelhütte (3340m) Located west of Saas-Fee, this hut is the third-highest SAC hut in Switzerland. It has 130 beds and is open mid June to mid September. Mischabelhütte AACZ,

CH-3906 Saas-Fee. Tel +41 27 957 13 17 / +41 79 835 20 72, mischabelhuette@gmail.com, www.mischabelhutte.ch

Britanniahütte (3030m) Situated south of Saas-Almagell, this hut has 134 beds and is open late June to end of September. Britannia Hütte SAC, CH-3906 Saas-Fee. Tel +41 27 957 22 88, info@britannia.ch, www.britannia.ch

Berghotel Almagelleralp (2200m) This hut provides accommodation in rooms and dormitories and is open mid June to mid October. Berghotel Almagelleralp, CH-3905 Saas-Almagell. Tel +41 79 629 78 08, info@almagelleralp.ch, www.almagelleralp.com

Almagellerhütte (2894m) Located on the south side of the Weissmies, this hut has 120 beds, plus group accommodation for 28 people, and is open mid June to end of September. Almagellerhütte, Hugo Anthamatten, CH-3905 Saas-Almagell. Tel +41 27 957 11 79 www.almagellerhuette.ch

Weissmieshütte (2726m) Situated high above Saas-Grund, this hut has 130 beds and is open mid June to late September. Weissmieshütte, CH-3910 Saas-Grund. Tel +41 27 957 25 54, huette@weissmieshuette.ch, www.weissmieshuette.ch

In addition, the Monte Moro Hut, **Rifugio Oberto Maroli**, 2796m, is located just over the Monte Moro col in Italy. It is open at all times when the summer lift from Macugnaga is operating, and it has 32 beds.

As well as huts, there are mountain restaurants at Hannig, Gletschergrotte, Spielboden, Längflue, Felskinn, Mattmark, Furggstalden, Heidbodme, and Kreuzboden.

OTHER MOUNTAIN ACTIVITIES

Saas-Fee has several via ferratas: the Jägihorn above Kreuzboden and the Mittaghorn above Plattjen. Additionally, a ferrata route climbs the Sasservispa Gorge from Unter den Bodmen to Saas-Fee. As the route passes through the Saaservispa gorge, a mountain guide is essential as there have been fatalities.

In addition, a range of other mountain activities are popular, including climbing the 4000m peaks around the valley, some of which are regarded as straightforward – the Allalinhorn, Weissmies and Lagginhorn in particular. Others, such as the Täschhorn and Dom, are much harder. Mountain biking is possible but most bikers congregate in Zermatt.

WALK 31

Fee, Almagell, Grund and the
Feevispa gorge

Start/finish	Saas-Fee, 1800m
Alternative finish	Saas-Almagell, 1670m, or Saas-Grund, 1560m
Distance	9km
Total ascent/descent	350m
Grade	1
Time	2hr–2hr 30min
Max altitude	1800m
Refreshments	Saas-Fee, Bodmen, Saas-Almagell, Saas-Grund
Access	Postbus to or from any of the villages

This easy circular walk visits all three of the main villages in the valley. It can also be started and finished in any of the villages, and the option via the lower gorge bridge provides good views into the deeper recesses of the Feevispa gorge, making an interesting variant.

The Kapellenweg is a short but interesting walk up through lightly wooded hillside, passing 15 large shrines before reaching the Maria zur Hohen Stiege chapel just below Saas-Fee. Allow at least an hour for this part of the route. A final shrine can be found just above the chapel. A more detailed description of the Kapellenweg is given in Walk 40. In order to follow the story of Christ in chronological order, it is best to walk the Kapellenweg from Saas-Grund to Saas-Fee. The terrace of the restaurant at Bodmen enjoys superb views of the lower Saastal.

From the tourist office in Saas-Fee, walk towards the bus station but then descend past the Wellness Hotel and follow the road as it curves left to cross the Panorama Bridge over the gorge. At the end of the road bridge take the smaller road left (still metalled) gently up, and at a path junction, continue ahead. (The path to the right angles back and is signed to the Felskinn cable car station.) The road now becomes a broad and easy track that

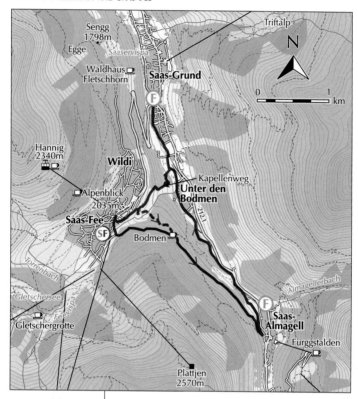

gently descends through light woodland all the way to Saas-Almagell.

After 10min you will pass the **Bodmen restaurant** on the left, which has a large terrace enjoying superb views down into the valley towards Saas-Grund and to the mountains north above Saas-Fee. Continue on down the track and after about 30min Saas-Almagell comes into view. You will then reach a path junction by a bridge. To proceed into the village, cross the bridge, passing a mini-golf area on the left, to emerge into **Saas-Almagell** village (1672m, 45min) by the information centre.

Saas-Almagell, the smallest of the three villages, has a number of older traditional houses and grain stores, as well as hotels of every standard.

To continue to Saas-Grund, at the path junction by the bridge follow the riverside path, with the river on your right, through lightly wooded areas. Occasionally, this path joins small roads, but this is never a problem. Continue through **Unter den Bodmen**, then cross the stream and continue on the riverside path all the way to **Saas-Grund** (1560m, 1hr 30min). ▶

Saas-Grund enjoys a key position in the valley, with transport links in all directions and a fine selection of shops, restaurants and accommodation. There is also a gondola service to Kreuzboden and Hohsaas.

From the tourist office in Saas-Grund take the road in the direction of Saas-Fee, cross the bridge over the river and immediately turn left down a slope to rejoin the riverside track. Walk south beside the river, and you will soon come to a pleasant campsite on your right, at the end of which there is a path junction. Take the right-hand path signed **Kapellenweg**. ▶ The path begins to climb almost immediately, but progress is steady on a good path mostly comprising flat stones in the form of rough steps.

The climb is never short of interest, with small shrines telling the life story of Christ every 100 metres or so. Continue on the distinct path and after about 40min you will reach a chapel perched on the hillside. The path continues beyond the chapel. The tremendous Saas Alpine gorge with the **Feevispa river** below can be seen to the left, and views open up ahead towards the glaciers and snowy peaks of the Lenzspitze, Dom, Täschhorn and Alphubel. After a further 5–10min you will emerge onto the large terrace of the Wellness Hotel in **Saas-Fee** (1800m, 2hr 30min)

If you do not wish to visit Saas-Grund, you can access the start of the Kapellenweg by turning left about 500 metres after Unter den Bodmen, immediately before the Kapellenweg campsite.

Further information on the Kapellenweg can be found in Walk 31.

One of the shrines on the Kapellenweg

Gorge path from Kapellenweg to Bodmen

This short extension walk is full of interest and takes an extra 30–45min. The views into the gorge from the footbridge crossing are spectacular, with huge rock outcrops squeezing the Feevispa river as it plummets down into the main valley. A woodland walk follows, then an opportunity to enjoy a drink or meal at the Waldhüs Bodmen restaurant, which has one of the best views down into the Saastal.

Begin the walk by descending the first part of the Kapellenweg, accessed from the terrace of the Wellness Hotel near the bus station. Just before the chapel turn right, signed 'Bodmen 25min'.

A sign by the bridge warns that access to the gorge via ferrata is only allowed with an official guide.

Descend the path to the bridge for some fantastic views down into the gorge. ◀ Once across the bridge, follow the path, which is fairly steep at first, up out of the gorge. The woodland path soon levels and then descends

The Saaservispa gorge

slightly, with a reassuring sign to **Bodmen**. Cross a meadow towards old farm buildings and a chalet, then finally climb directly to the restaurant. ▶

To return to **Saas-Fee**, turn right up the track and you will arrive over the Panorama Bridge in 15min. Turn right for the tourist office.

Bodmen also seems to be home to a variety of farm animals – geese, ducks, alpacas to name a few!

173

WALK 32
Hannig from Saas-Fee

Start/finish	Saas-Fee, 1800m
Distance	9km
Total ascent/descent	560m
Grade	2
Time	3hr 30min
Max altitude	2340m at Hannig
Refreshments	Hannig station has a restaurant; Hannigalp buvette is 200m below the station and the Alpenblick restaurant is 300m below

Hannig is a cable car station and restaurant situated north-west of Saas-Fee. It enjoys panoramic views over the Saas-Fee bowl and towards the icy peaks of the Mischabel range, as well as the Weissmies and Lagginhorn to the east.

It is quite possible to take the gondola up to Hannig and back down again. But it is also a good walk in its own right. The Hannig gondola is also one end of the Gemsweg tour of the Saas valley (Walk 35) and the start point of the ascent of Mällig (Walk 33), so during refurbishment it may only be possible to start these routes by walking up to Hannigalp.

The route takes in a couple of mountain restaurants so is well supplied with food as well as views. The climb passes through the woods above Saas-Fee and onto the open mountainside above, while the descent forms long steady zigzags down through the woods.

Saas-Fee can be confusing at first, but yellow signposts and elegant town signs will help you to head out of town in the right direction.

◄ From the tourist office and bus station, drop down into town and turn left at the Dom Hotel and pass the main church with its unique tower and steeple. Turn right immediately after the church onto Oberegasse. Follow this small road as it climbs steeply, passing a left fork and then a right fork. The road becomes wider as it passes chalets and the Schäferstube restaurant and heads through a triangle of pines. The path is unclear here, passing either

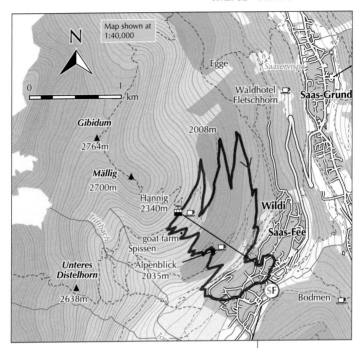

left, right or, as recommended, through the pines, but all options lead to the main route. At a track junction a path to the Mischabelhütte is signed. Don't take this path. Instead, turn right and take a path to the left and upwards signed to Hannig and the Alpenblick restaurant.

Follow the signs to the Alpenblick through several turns. The **Alpenblick** (2035m, 45min–1hr) is a well-known mountain restaurant and in places the path has been equipped with unnecessary cables, presumably to help diners up or maybe down! ▶

Climb above the restaurant, now following signs to Hannig. Several paths lead the same way, so keep heading upwards to reach the edge of the forest at 2120m, 15min after leaving the restaurant. Pass through a gate labelled 'Please don't feed the goats' and continue to

Views across the Sass valley from the restaurant are extensive.

175

Looking up to the Mischabel peaks from the route to Hannig

climb to the **Hannigalp goat farm** (2155m), where there may also be a summer buvette.

Continue climbing the zigzag path, and you will soon arrive at **Hannig** (2340m, 1hr 30min–2hr).

> **Hannig** is the start point for several routes so any closure of the cable car will mean hikers will have to walk up instead. The mountain restaurant has a substantial terrace that looks out over the entire valley and its surrounding peaks. The *früchtekuche* is also excellent.

Although on the map this looks like a long series of hairpin bends, which it is, the route is very pleasant, with views above the treeline and welcome shade on hot summer days.

The descent route to Saas-Fee follows tracks and paths on a steady, easy gradient all the way down. ◄ The final path leads into Saas-Fee, coming out at the Hannig bottom gondola station.

To descend to the Hannig bottom gondola station, take the path to the right behind the Hannig top station (2340m), signed 'Saas-Fee 1hr 20min'. For the most part the route follows a track, but occasionally it switches to paths. Descend on the track for 30min to 2215m, then leave the track briefly and head right down a path until you meet the track again. Continue down the track to **2008m** at a hairpin bend, where a signed path indicates the direction of the *höhenweg* to Grächen (1hr from Hannig).

Continue round the hairpin bend but shortly afterwards take a left-hand fork onto an old mule track. This track runs parallel to the main track above and leads down to a junction of paths by a small pond. Keep the pond to your right and at a path signpost by a large rock take a left-hand turn signed to Saas-Fee. Almost immediately this path swings sharply right and descends easily. The first chalet buildings soon appear, and the path swings left then immediately right to become a small tarmac road. Just as you pass under the cables of the Hannig gondola, turn sharp left, then immediately sharp right on a small zigzag path through meadows to arrive at the Hannig bottom gondola station.

Head downhill into the town centre, keep right and then left at the Dom Hotel to return to the start point at the **Saas-Fee** tourist office (1800m, 3hr 30min).

WALK 33
The ascent of Mällig – The Ibex Trail

Start	Hannig gondola station, 2340m
Finish	Saas-Fee, 1800m
Distance	9km
Total ascent	420m
Total descent	960m
Grade	3
Time	4hr
Max altitude	Gibidum at 2764m on the ridge above Mällig
Refreshments	Hannig gondola station, Waldhotel Fletschhorn at Egge near the finish and Saas-Fee
Access	To return to Hannig take the gondola from Saas-Fee

This easily accessible mountain route is one of the best walks in the valley. It is referred to locally as the Ibex Trail – there is a good chance you will see some of these beautiful mountain inhabitants during your walk. After a straightforward ascent to Mällig, the route follows a ridge with 360° views across to the Weissmies and Lagginhorn, north to the Rhône valley and, nearer at hand, to the Lenzspitze and Nadelhorn, as well as the Saas-Fee bowl.

The ridge above Mällig is mainly broad and straightforward, apart from a steep section near Gletscherweng, where the route rejoins the *höhenweg* path to Saas-Fee. Under snow, parts of the route could turn into a mountaineering expedition, so this route is best tackled when there is no snow on the ground.

If the Hannig gondola is closed, the climb from Saas-Fee to Hannig (see Walk 32), is very pleasant and takes 1hr 30min to 2hr, making this a full day walk.

From the Hannig gondola station turn right and climb the easy zigzags to the summit of Mällig. At 2550m, pass a grassy platform with spectacular views of the Dom; the climb then becomes rockier and slightly steeper, passing through substantial avalanche defences to reach the summit of **Mällig** (2700m, 50min–1hr), which turns out not to be the high point.

Continue along the rocky crest. At no point is it narrow or exposed, although the drops to your left are certainly impressive. After 10min you will pass a signpost suggesting Saas-Fee is 2hr 30min away.

After this rocky section cross a broad plateau, before climbing easily to the high point at **Gibidum** (2764m, 1hr 30min).

The views from all parts of the ridge are outstanding, but **Gibidum** is perhaps the best viewpoint of all. Views extend north to the Bernese Alps and south to the Italian border and the Monte Moro Pass, so this is one of the best places to study the eastern wall of the Saastal. Above, the Lenzspitze and the famed ice slope on its north-east face can clearly be seen.

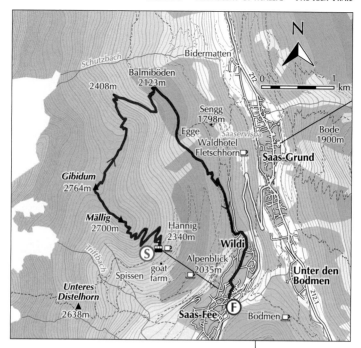

The descent route drops in stages. Facing north, it may hold snow well into July, but you can usually walk around old *névés*. After several 'steps' down you will come to a steeper boulder and scree section before the walking becomes easier below **2408m**.

There remains one gully to cross, which can be awkward in snow, but once past this obstacle the route drops in zigzags to join the Grächen Höhenweg path at Balmiboden (2123m); Saas-Fee is 1hr 10min from here. Follow the route now signed all the way into Saas-Fee, taking care with any route changes close to the **Waldhotel Fletschhorn** at Egge, perhaps a suitable place for a break before the finish. Continue on the track and pass through **Wildi**, a 'suburb' of **Saas-Fee**, before walking into the centre, turning left for the tourist office (1800m, 4hr).

WALK 34
Gletschergrotte, Spielboden and Längflue

Start	Saas-Fee, 1800m
Finish	Spielboden, 2448m
Alternative finish	Längflue, 2869m
Distance	4.5km (alternative 6.5k)
Total ascent	690m (alternative 1110m)
Total descent	40m (alternative 40m)
Grade	2 (3 if continued to Längflue)
Time	2hr 15min ascent time (alternative 3hr 30min)
Max altitude	2448m at Spielboden (2869m at Längflue)
Refreshments	Gletschergrotte restaurant; Spielboden; Längflue
Note	If you plan to descend by gondola, check the times of the last descents before setting out.

A gentle walk across the Saas-Fee bowl leads to Gletschergrotte, a fine mountain restaurant, before a climb leads to Spielbodenalp and a second mountain restaurant. If desired, a further climb will take you to yet another restaurant at Längflue; with careful timing you can dine well on this route! As this walk passes under the Mischabel mountains, the views upwards are foreshortened. The higher points of the route bring you close to the glaciers, while the Weissmies and Lagginhorn are outlined to the east across the Saastal, and Saas-Fee appears in miniature far below.

The route presents few difficulties up to Spielboden, although the path becomes steep. Above Spielboden the route is even steeper, becoming a Grade 3. Late snow would make the walk more challenging so don't attempt Längflue until summer is well set.

It is possible to walk back down to Saas-Fee, but you may prefer to save your knees by taking the gondola, as recommended in the route description. However, should you wish to walk back down, it will take 2hr 30min from Längflue and 1hr 30min from Spielboden.

From the tourist office walk through the centre of Saas-Fee in the direction of the church. About 200 metres beyond

the church fork right on a path signed to Gletschergrotte. The path almost immediately leaves the town, crossing a large meadow. Fork left and cross a stream, then take the right-hand path signed to Gletschersee and Gletschergrotte. Continue following signs, climbing over a large wooded moraine, with the Feevispa to your left, to reach a path junction. Descend to cross a bridge and turn left (1910m, 45min). The **Gletschersee** is to your right; it is no longer a distinct pool, as the entire area has become silted with the river forming multiple braiding channels.

Shortly after, fork half left just below a gondola pylon. Climb towards this and swing right to continue up on a path through the wood. At a junction turn right to arrive a minute later at the superbly situated **Gletschergrotte** restaurant (1998m, 1hr).

Spielboden, the next stop on the walk, is a further 450m above the valley, which will take 1hr 15min. Retrace your steps from the restaurant for 30 metres then take the turn up to the right. Zigzag steeply uphill through bushes and small trees, with summer flowers on the ground, and after 15min you will pass a summer farm on

The Gletschersee is more a series of braids than a single lake

181

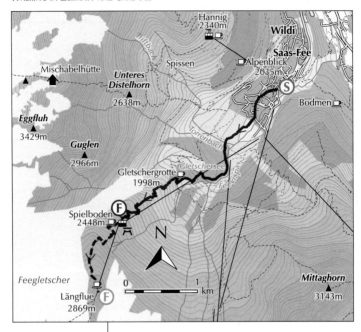

This lush green grass can be spotted from many places in the Saas valley.

a small pasture. ◄ Climb steadily as the vegetation turns to rockier ground and after 30min cross a ski piste.

> The deep trough gouged by the **Feegletscher** is to the right, and it is a very impressive sight. The earthmoving capabilities of the glaciers doubtless strike real envy at Caterpillar's offices. It is possible, although steep, to climb the piste and look down onto the remains of the glacier and its debris.

Cross the piste and then climb on the path that follows close to the route of the Spielboden gondola above before emerging at the top of the lift and the **Mountain Restaurant Spielboden** (2448m, 2hr 15min). From here, you can either take the gondola back down or carry on further to Längflue.

At Längflue you are in amongst the Dom's glaciers

Continuation to Längflue

Only continue to Längflue when the snow has (largely) melted and conditions are settled. The climb to Längflue is a further 420m, which takes over an hour. It's not far but the path takes you over 2800m, and it is steeper than the climb to Spielboden. ▸

To continue to Längflue take a path that heads right from the Spielboden gondola station. It soon heads left and climbs steeply up the nose of the hill above Spielboden before joining a concreted piste through a narrow notch in rocks with orange protective barriers.

Continue over steadily rising rockier terrain and follow close to the line of a ski lift. The path narrows before climbing a short steep section on rocks (difficult if snow-covered), which is protected by cables, and continues to the **Längflue** top station (2869m, 3hr 30min)

The highlight of the route is the impressive Mischabel mountain wall ahead rather than the ski tracks you follow, so you may prefer to take the gondola up instead, which opens at the end of June.

Längflue top station sits close under the Dom and its glaciers, which rise impressively above. It has a café with comfy seating and enjoys 360° views. Five minutes above the station a small snow lake carrying icebergs well into the summer makes an interesting short excursion.

To return to Saas-Fee, take the gondolas, which will take about 20min, changing at Spielboden and the Felskinn bottom station. If you prefer to walk down, reverse the route; this will take about 2hr 30min (1hr to Spielboden and 1hr 30min from Spielboden to Saas-Fee).

WALK 35

The Gemsweg – a tour of the Saas-Fee valley

Start	Saas-Fee, 1800m
Alternative start	Plattjen, 2570m
Finish	Hannig, 2340m
Distance	14km (alternative 8km)
Total ascent	830m (alternative 660m)
Total descent	830m (alternative 430m)
Grade	2–3
Time	4hr 30min; alternative 3hr 30min
Max altitude	2570m at Plattjen
Refreshments	Gletschergrotte restaurant, Hannigalp, Alpenblick restaurant, Hannig restaurant
Access	By gondola to Hannig or Plattjen (if operational)

The Gemsweg, one of the great walks of the Saas valley, contours intricately around Saas's high mountain bowl, among the crashing glacial torrents outflowing from the Feegletscher, dropping towards the valley floor but never quite getting there. Views of the Mischabel wall above are ever-present, and across the valley the mountains to the east are seen to best effect. Several well-sited mountain inns provide refreshments, making it possible to organise your day so that lunch may be taken at the Gletschergrotte restaurant, followed by dessert at Hannig – or tea if your pace is slower.

There are few route-finding issues as the route is well signed, often as the Gemsweg; however, there are short, cabled sections on either side of the valley, some of the hillsides are steep and the route passes through an area of boulders just below Gletschergrotte.

The route can be walked in either direction, but if the Plattjen gondola is not operating, it is better to start from Saas-Fee and finish at the restaurant in Hannig (or the Alpenblick), as described here. If it is operating, the full Plattjen–Hannig (or vice versa) tour (outlined in the alternative start) can easily be done and is, in fact, shorter with less ascent, as the gondolas remove some of the hard work. Likewise, if the Hannig gondola is not operating, you can descend directly on foot to Saas-Fee.

The first half of the route from Saas-Fee to Gletschergrotte takes 2hr 30min, climbing the hillside south of Saas-Fee and contouring to the head of the valley.

Alternative start from Plattjen

If the Plattjen gondola is running, start from the top station and descend to the (currently closed) Berghaus Plattjen (15min). Turn left under the cable car line and descend gradually to join the main route at the **2190m** path junction.

Alternatively, it is quite possible to walk from Saas-Fee to Plattjen (see Walk 37).

From the Saas-Fee bus station and tourist office drop down and bear left over the Panorama Bridge, a substantial construction more suitable for a motorway than a mountain resort. Turn left and after a short climb turn sharp right on a path labelled '**Bodmenwasserleitung**', running alongside the leat. It is a beautiful path just above the valley floor with the gurgling water at your feet. Pass under an aerial ropeway course and by a picnic spot, and almost to the **Felskinn** station.

Before the station turn left on a path, shared with Walk 37, that zigzags up the small piste. The route climbs along the edge of the piste, crosses a track and continues

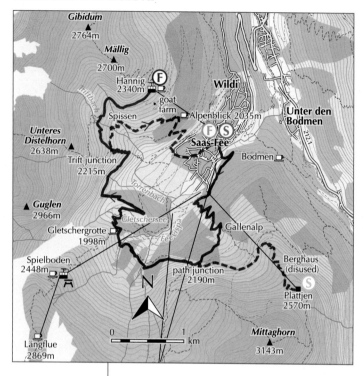

up, sometimes through woods and sometimes in the open, with flowers and alpenrose for company. Take the first turn to the right at buildings at **Gallenalp** and finally cross the open piste and climb through woods to a path junction at **2190m** (1hr 30min).

Turn right towards Gletschergrotte. The path descends almost immediately, passes an attractive waterfall and then narrows with a couple of cabled sections. Cross the infant **Feevispa**, a major outflow from the Feegletscher, on a good bridge, then cross a ski piste, another stream and a second piste and take the track up to **Gletschergrotte** (1998m, 2hr 30min).

Gletschergrotte is a superbly sited mountain restaurant with views down the valley. The Spielboden
gondola purrs almost silently close by. Spielboden
is a further 1hr walk uphill from here, while the
walk back down to Saas-Fee would also take 1hr.

The next section of the route climbs high on the
western side of the Saas-Fee bowl, crossing mountain
streams and making its way to the Hannig restaurant and
gondola in 2hr. To continue, leave the Gletschergrotte
restaurant on the path heading north (the path runs
through the restaurant). Follow this and descend 100m,
threading through boulders to join the glacial outflows.
Here there are higher and lower routes; the higher route
is a bit rockier and the direct, lower route is easier.

Follow the streams down, crossing two bridges, then
climb diagonally up onto the moraine wall. Turn sharp
left and climb the crest of the moraine. ▶

After 750 metres on the moraine, the path turns sharp
right to cross above rocks and over a stream. This section
is protected by cables. The path climbs the steep hillside
to a 2073m path junction where it joins the path to the

*Crossing the
infant Feevispa*

The glacial
torrents draining
the Mischabel
peaks above crash
noisily before
merging into the
meandering waters
that lie increasingly
far below.

187

If the Hannig gondola is not operating, you may prefer to take the alternative direct descent to Saas-Fee outlined below.

Mischabelhütte. Turn left and climb steeply in zigzags to the **Trift path junction** at 2215m. ◄

From the Trift junction continue ahead, descending gradually to cross a large stream draining the Hohbalmgletscher at **Spissen**, then contour to cross a second smaller stream. Climb a slanting path under rocks to reach a corner and walk on level ground to **Hannig** (2340m, 4hr 30min). From Hannig, take the gondola down to **Saas-Fee**.

Direct descent to Saas-Fee

If the Hannig gondola is not operating, you can descend directly to Saas-Fee from the Trift junction by crossing two streams to reach the **goat farm** at Hannigalp. Here, take the twisting path into the forest (reversing the ascent in Route 32), passing the **Alpenblick restaurant** (2035m). Descend in more zigzags to eventually emerge in **Saas-Fee**.

WALK 36

The Mischabelhütte

Start/finish	Saas-Fee, 1800m
Alternative start/finish	Hannig, 2340m
Distance	12km
Total ascent/descent	1600m
Grade	4
Time	7–8hr
Max altitude	3335m at the Mischabelhütte
Refreshments	Mischabelhütte
Access	The alternative start/finish at Hannig is accessed by the Hannig gondola
Warning	Suitable only for walkers comfortable with the level of exposure found in the high mountains. This hard, high route has ferrata-like protection towards the top. Do not attempt if lightning is forecast.

The climb to the Mischabelhütte is one of the highest routes in the region, and it is challenging; it takes you into a high mountain environment, normally the preserve of the climber. After climbing steeply for the first 1000m, the route heads onto rocks on a steep path protected by cables, metal steps and ladders as it climbs the ridge to the hut.

This is a route for a fine day; it is long and steep and takes almost as much time to descend as it does to climb. Therefore, an overnight in the hut would be a good option, returning the next morning. Start early in settled conditions and be prepared to turn back if the weather changes. The upper section of the route is arguably harder to contemplate than to actually do, but if you are not confident, be prepared to turn back; the 2806m Distelhorn is a good spot to make this call, at the end of the steep and surprisingly good path.

The Mischabelhütte is the start point for climbs on the Nadelhorn and Lenzspitze (and the less climbed Ulrichshorn), so you will be sharing the route with climbers who will be descending in the late morning from climbs, most commonly the Nadelgrat. This walk is a high mountain route, as close as any walker will get to these peaks, and there is scenery to match.

From the Saas-Fee tourist office drop down and walk through the centre of town to the church. Immediately after the main church, with its modernist steeple, take a

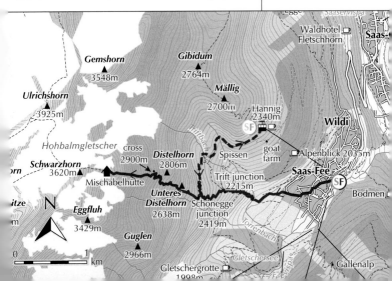

small road off to the right (Oberegasse) and climb past houses. The path leads through a commemorative stand of conifers (although other paths pass either side of these) and comes to the first blue sign for the Mischabelhütte (20min).

Pass through restored sheep pens, cross a small piste and walk under a bridge. Cross another, larger, piste and immediately after the top of a ski lift, just as the path starts to descend, seek out a right turn. ◄ Cross a bridge and you will come to the start of the real climb (30min from Saas-Fee).

At the time of writing this is waymarked but not signed.

The path rises at a steep but manageable angle, joining the Gletschergrotte–Hannig path at 2070m as far as the 2215m **Trift path junction**. Take the path that continues up to the **Schönegge path junction** at 2419m (1hr 35min). Signs indicate 2hr 30min to the hut. From this point the path becomes a blue alpine trail. ◄

The path to and from Hannig, which may be used as an alternative ascent or descent, joins here.

The already steep path, if anything, steepens at this point, but not by much. Considering the mountainsides it is crossing, it is a remarkably good path, so in good conditions its alpine nature is disguised for a long time. Keep heading up. At 2650m there is a potentially awkward gully to cross, and at 2700m watch for a turn to the right (another path heads straight on but this is not the best route).

Walkers low down on the climb towards the hut

Climb to a notch in the ridge at 2750m. Shortly after, close to the **Distelhorn** (2806m, 2hr 30min), the route turns into a true mountain path that heads over rocks with protective steps and cables, so if you don't enjoy these, this is the point at which to decide whether to carry on or turn back.

A cable stretches out right towards the ridge. Continue on cables and stemples to aid your ascent over rock steps and large boulders. Look out for the blue-and-white paint that marks the route. Occasionally, the path descends slightly before regaining the ridge. This is clearly marked with blue-and-white paint but keep looking out for it, as it is easy to carry on up the ridge if too focused on the climbing. At around 2900m there is a **cross** situated on the ridge. It is at this section that the route is most precarious. Beyond this point the route continues steeply but the route finding is more straightforward. Plentiful cables and stemples aid both route finding and the ascent. The hut, perched on its rocky outcrop, never seems to get closer. Eventually, you will gain the final section and the steps to the terrace of the **Mischabelhütte** (3335m) in around 4hr–4hr 30min.

THE MISCHABELHÜTTE

The Mischabelhütte is perched at 3335m on a small rocky outcrop between the Hohbalm and Fall glaciers. Owned by the Academic Alpine Club of Zurich, it is the third highest SAC hut in Switzerland. The original hut was built in 1904 and could accommodate 42 climbers. With its popularity growing considerably over the years, an additional larger building and outbuildings were constructed in 1976, now providing a total of 130 beds. The hut is used by mountaineers to access the Lenzspitze, the Nadelhorn, the Ulrichshorn and the Hohberghorn at the northern end of the Mischabel range. The views down the valley and to the surrounding peaks just 2km away are breathtaking!

Descend the same route, taking care throughout. The top section will take as long to descend as it did to climb up, although the path below 2750m is good for a speedier descent, assuming your knees can cope.

Alternative start from Hannig

This option can be used to ascend or descend the route, saving 30min walking in either direction and over 400m of ascent.

From the Hannig gondola turn left and continue along a level path to a corner, then descend under rocks and cross the Torrenbach stream. Turn another corner and drop to **Spissen**, cross the Triftbach stream, taking the higher path signed 'Schönegge and Mischabel'. Climb 120m to reach **Schönegge** (2420m, 40min) to join the main route.

If returning to Hannig, take the signed left turn at Schönegge and reverse the route back to the gondola.

WALK 37
Plattjen

Start/finish	Saas-Fee, 1800m
Distance	8km
Total ascent/descent	780m
Grade	2
Time	4hr: 2hr 30min up and 1hr 30min down
Max altitude	Plattjen (2570m)
Refreshments	Saas-Fee
Note	If the Plattjen lift is operating and the restaurants are open, this route becomes much more popular.

Plattjen is the start point for routes to the Britanniahütte and the Mittaghorn, although in some seasons the gondola and restaurant may be closed. Despite this, the walk is good and it is an excellent viewpoint, a sentinel matching Hannig across the valley. For those planning to walk around the Egginer and Britanniahütte or those doing the Mittaghorn via ferrata, this walk will provide you with the ascent and descent routes needed.

There are no route-finding problems or difficulties with the terrain, but it is a climb of nearly 800m, so it is likely to take 2hr 30min.

The route starts low down in pleasant woods, which make for cool walking even on hot summer days, and climbs onto open mountainside, where flowers thrive and shrubs and trees are repopulating the pistes. The views from Plattjen are all that you could imagine, especially down the Saastal and to the mountains beyond the Rhône valley. For views to the south towards the Mattmark continue a little way above Plattjen, sampling the mountain path under the Mittaghorn. The route descends below the *berghotel*, before joining a forest track for the final stretch into Saas-Fee.

From the Saas-Fee tourist office, head downhill and keep left across the Panorama Bridge. Continue on the small tarmac road to the right. Pass the Alpin Express gondola station and the **Spielboden/Plattjen gondola**. Continue for 200 metres and take a path on the left that climbs

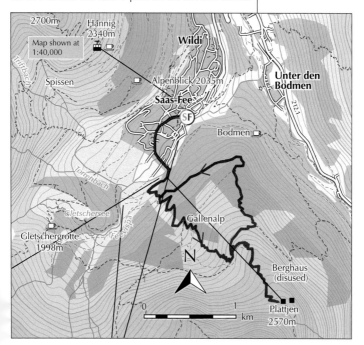

steeply, initially at the bottom of a piste. (You can also reach this route by turning left just after the bridge, taking the next right on the leat path, the Bodmenwasserleitung, and following this through woods above, joining the route at the first track crossed.)

Climb steeply on this path and cross the leat path. Continue up and cross another track; this is used on the descent. Climb in and out of forest on a good path, passing the old buildings of **Gallenalp** (2061m), where a right turn to Gletschergrotte and Egginerjoch is signed (this path is taken on Walk 34), but keep left and climb to cross another track. Continue straight ahead. ◀

The path twists in and out of the forest, passing through alpenrose and small shrubs that are repopulating the hillside.

After 1hr 40min, you will reach another path junction at 2327m. Turn left and you will soon reach the (currently closed) **Berghaus Plattjen** (2411m, 2hr).

Take the path that climbs underneath the gondola cables for 1km and 150m to reach the **Plattjen gondola station** (2570m, 2hr 30min) and the end of the walk.

Beyond Plattjen the path heads to the Britanniahütte and the Egginerjoch, before returning to Felskinn, which is described in Walk 39 but in reverse.

REFORESTATION OF PLATTJEN AND HANNIG

The Saastal was heavily deforested during the construction of the railways, especially the nearby Susten Pass. This left the hillsides of Plattjen and Hannig right above Saas-Fee bare and exposed to avalanches. Such deforestation has led to many catastrophes, such as the avalanches that fell on Evolène in 1999 and 2010, but also on many other occasions across the Alps too. From the middle of the 20th century onwards, trees have been allowed to regrow, resulting in the forested mountainsides we see today and much reducing the risk of avalanches.

To descend, return to **Berghaus Plattjen** (20min) and retrace the ascent path down to the path junction (10min). Turn right signed for the Waldweg to Saas-Fee and Saas-Almagell. This track becomes a path with superb views down to Saas-Fee and the lower Saas valley, as well as the surrounding peaks, and across to

Hannig. After a further 10–15min you will reach another path junction. Take the left-hand path that indicates 1hr 15min to Saas-Fee.

This is a good path that zigzags steeply down through beautiful woods. After 30min you will reach a track. Turn right and follow the now gently descending track for 1.3km. At a clearing (ski piste), with the **Felskinn station** ahead of you, turn right onto the small path used on the initial stage of the ascent route and descend. The leat path can be seen on the right heading into woods, but if preferred, continue down to the track below. Turn right and walk back into **Saas-Fee** (1800m, 4hr).

The old berghotel at Plattjen is now closed

WALK 38
The Britanniahütte by the glacier route

Start	Mattmark 2204m
Finish	The Britanniahütte 3028m
Distance	7km
Total ascent	950m
Total descent	120m
Grade	4
Time	3hr 30min
Max altitude	3028m at the Britanniahütte Hut
Refreshments	None until the Britanniahütte Hut
Access	Bus to Mattmark

The straightforward glacier crossing can be used to get to the well-known Britanniahütte or to return to the valley. Check that the crossing is open on the hut's website but normally it will be in summer. It's a blue alpine route, arguably at the easier end of the scale, but as a glacier crossing in a high mountain environment it should be treated with all due care. If there has been substantial snowfall, it's better to wait for the glacier to dry, so that any crevasses can be seen clearly. Substantial boulder moraines may well prove to be more challenging than the glaciers.

In terms of gear it's claimed that none is necessary and this is indeed valid, but the inexperienced glacier crosser will feel happier with either crampons or micro spikes. The routes are well marked and trodden.

Save the route for good weather. In sunny conditions a traverse is straightforward, but if visibility is poor it could be a stern test of navigation skills on both glaciers and the moraine, besides which, it would be a great shame not to see the surrounding mountain views, which are some of the best and closest in the region.

From the Mattmark bus stop walk along the west shore of the **Mattmark** reservoir. After 10min find a well-marked turn to the right and begin to climb on a good track. After 5min a short cut climbs steeply on the right, but it's easier

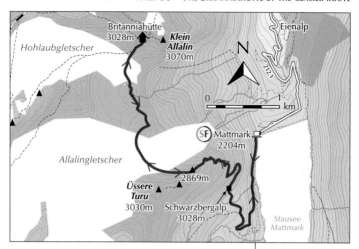

to stay on the track. Follow the track as it makes a loop to the right and pass signs for the Seejinenberg ridge and then the route taken in Walk 48. Follow the track as it bears right before coming to the farm buildings at **Schwarzbergalp** (2380m, 45min).

Take the path to the left of the building and start to climb. ▶ After half way up the climb the path becomes easier and you soon come to the summit of the **Schwarzbergkopf** (2869m, 2hr 10min).

The path is narrow and may feel slightly exposed in a couple of places as it climbs the bulky buttresses.

> The 360-degree **views from the Schwarzbergkopf** are spectacular, from the reservoir far below, the glaciers tumbling down from the Strahlhorn and Rimpfischhorn above and the two glaciers ahead with the Britannia Hut perched on its notch in the Allalinhorn ridge.

From the summit take the signed path down to the **Allalingletscher**. This becomes steadily rougher as it crosses the moraine. The first steps on the glacier are rock covered and straightforward as far as a medial moraine part way across. After this the glacier is ice and snow, and if you want

Looking across the Allalingletscher from the summit of Schwarzbergkopf

to use spikes, here is the place to gear up. Continue across, following tracks and marker posts, until you reach a substantial pile of moraine debris, and ungear here.

Follow the frequent blue signs across the rocky moraine. Initially these may be sparse, but veer slightly right to find the route. It's slow going across the moraine, but after 15min it levels out into glacier-ironed slabs that are much easier and guide your descent to the **Hohlaubgletscher**. This is shorter to cross but again you may prefer crampons.

After the glacier, face up to another moraine bank with large rocks to surmount, follow the blue marks carefully as even 3m off route makes the going much harder, before finding a good path that climbs just below rocks and above grass to reach the **Britanniahütte** (3028m, 3hr 30min).

THE BRITANNIAHÜTTE

The Britanniahütte is one of the most visited huts in the Alps. Its original construction was funded by the Association of British Members of the Swiss Alpine Club (ABMSAC). The original hut was assembled in Geneva and carried up the mountain from Saas Almagell.

With accommodation for 130, its well worth spending the night there. It is used by climbers on some of the Allalinhorn routes, as well as a popular via ferrata on the cliffs immediately above the hut.

Return can be either reversing the route to Mattmark, or reversing Walk 39 to Plattjen, but check the time of the last cablecar from Plattjen and the last bus from Mattmark as the walk down the Saas Fee takes nearly 1hr 30min. Descent via the Egginerjoch is also possible (see Walk 39).

The Britanniahütte with June snow

WALK 39
The Britanniahütte from Plattjen

Start	Plattjen, 2570m
Finish	The Britanniahütte, 3028m
Alternative finish	Plattjen gondola station, 2570m
Distance	5km
Total ascent	170m
Total descent	100m
Grade	3/4
Time	2hr 30min
Max altitude	3028m at the Britanniahütte Hut
Refreshments	None until the Britanniahütte Hut
Access	Gondola from Saas Fee to Plattjen

The route from the Plattjen gondola station to the Britanniahütte makes one of the finest walks in the region, a justifiably popular challenge. Save the route for good weather as the scenery is magnificent – south up the Stausee Mattmark, east to the Lagginhorn and Weissmies and, on the approach to the hut, to the Allalinhorn and then the Rimpfischhorn and Strahlhorn peaks seen from the hut.

The route skirts the slopes of the Mittaghorn and there are a couple of cabled sections with slight exposure. If visibility is poor and snow on the ground, navigation in the mountain bowl between the Egginer and the hut could be challenging, another reason to await fine weather.

Saas Fee to Plattjen

If the Plattjen lift is not running, or you wish to walk from Saas Fee, Take the route in Walk 37 from Saas, climbing 800m in around 2hr 30min. In descent, allow 1hr 30min.

From the **Plattjen gondola** (2570m) take the signed route south. Views to the east and south are outstanding, while the array of peaks above Saas Fee stand tall behind. The route is partly through boulders which are slow going and partly on a good path along wide ledges. Look down on the village of Saas Almagell 900m below.

Pass the Mittaghorn path (not for walkers) and continue round the boulder Meiggertal, coming to viewpoint at **Heidefridhof** (2763m). Continue on a narrow section with some cables for protection before entering the mountain bowl, joining with a path direct from Saas Almagell. A path direct to the Egginerjoch heads right, but keep left towards the hut, climbing a moraine before coming to a **path junction at 2863m** between small lakes. ◀

If visibility is poor, take great care on navigation here.

Here keep left again. Climb sloping slabs before crossing moraine and rubble to complete the climb to the **Britanniahütte** (3028m, 2hr 30min).

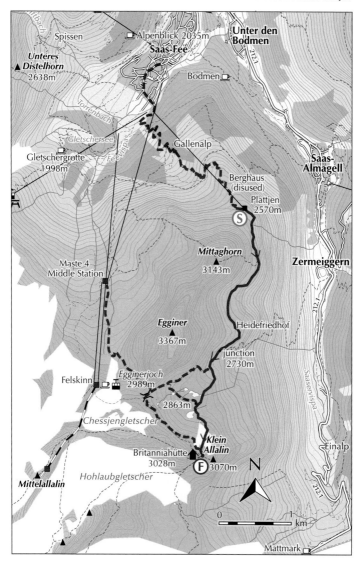

OPTIONS FROM THE BRITANNIAHÜTTE

- Return to Plattjen the same way. Allow 2hr, plus any descent time to Saas Fee if the gondolas are not running.

- Continue across the glaciers after the hut to the Schwarzbergkopf and Mattmark, reversing Walk 38. If doing this check conditions and plan ahead if you prefer crampons or microspikes. Allow 2hr 30min to 3hr.

- Return to the 2863m junction and climb to the Egginerjoch (2988m). There are fine views of the Saas peaks.

- From the Egginerjoch, descend to the middle cablecar station (Maste 4) at 2580m on the Felskinn lift.

The Mattmark from the trail to Plattjen

FELSKINN CABLECAR

A level path between the Felskinn station and the Egginerjoch gives easy access to the high mountain environment. But serious rockfall has closed the path and it is unclear whether and when it will be reopened. Check the hut website or with the tourist office to confirm if you wish to use this route. In early summer with plentiful snow, an almost level piste runs from the Egginerjoch to the hut.

WALK 40

Saas-Grund to Saas-Fee – the Kapellenweg and Saumweg

Start/finish	Saas-Grund, 1560m
Alternative finish	Saas-Fee, 1800m
Distance	4km
Total ascent/descent	250m
Grade	1
Time	1hr–1hr 30min
Max altitude	1748m (1800m if continuing to Saas-Fee)
Refreshments	Saas-Fee and Saas-Grund, but none en route

This circular walk explores the two main paths that link Saas-Grund with Saas-Fee. Until the road was completed in the early 1950s, these were the only routes linking the two villages. The Kapellenweg is full of interest, passing 15 shrines to reach a chapel that stands on a site overlooking the Feevispa gorge. Linking this chapel with another found on the Saumweg, the Meditativer Rundweg traverses the hillside through beautiful woods, threading a well-made path beneath rocky outcrops. Returning to Saas-Grund, the Saumweg (Alter Saumweg) is an ancient, cobbled mule track that serves as an evocative reminder of the old ways of travel – in the not- too-distant past, when it was the main route up to Saas-Fee.

The paths are all well made and maintained; however, care should be taken in wet conditions as the cobbles and bare rock slabs can become slippery.

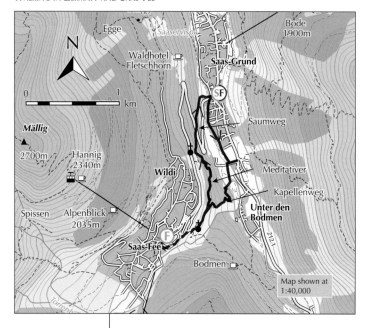

Beginning at the tourist information centre in Saas-Grund, cross the bridge on the Saas-Fee road and immediately turn left to walk beside the river. Pass a campsite, at the far end of which is a plaque on a large rock indicating the start of the **Kapellenweg** (10min).

You will reach the first shrine immediately, which depicts the annunciation of the Angel to Mary. Further shrines follow at regular intervals as you climb the hillside. The path is well made, although in wet conditions care should be taken on the rock slabs. After about 40min you will pass the last of the shrines and the **chapel** will come into view. ◄

Having viewed the chapel, retrace your steps downhill past one shrine, then look for a sign indicating the path to the Meditativer Rundweg to the left. This is a broad, well-made path that undulates through larch woods along flights of log steps as it picks its way below

To continue into Saas-Fee climb a flight of stone steps, then fork left to emerge a few minutes later on a large terraced area next to the Wellness Hotel.

THE KAPELLENWEG

A scene from one of the shrines along the Kapellenweg

Constructed between 1708 and 1711, the 15 shrines on the Kappellenweg depict the following:

- The Annunciation of the Angel to Mary
- The visitation of Mary to Saint Elizabeth
- The nativity of Jesus in Bethlehem
- The presentation of Jesus in the Temple
- The discovery of Jesus in the Temple
- The agony of Christ in the Garden
- The scourging of Christ at the pillar
- The crowning with thorns
- The carrying of the cross
- The crucifixion and death of Jesus
- The resurrection of Jesus Christ
- The ascension of Jesus into Heaven
- The descent of the Holy Spirit on the Apostles
- The assumption of the Blessed Virgin Mary into Heaven
- The coronation of the Blessed Virgin Mary in Heaven

The chapel, which predates the shrines, was completed in 1687, and an additional large porch area was completed in 1747. The interior of the chapel is very simple, save for an elaborate altarpiece typical of many Catholic churches in the area.

cliffs with the Saas-Fee road high above. Glimpses of Saas-Grund and the valley below are rewarding. After 10–15min the path rounds a prominent rock buttress and climbs to join the Alter Saumweg beside another **chapel**. Turn right to begin the descent to **Saas-Grund**.

The Alter Saumweg originates in Wildi outside Saas-Fee.

◄ Take the ancient cobbled mule track that descends moderately steeply for about 250 metres before reaching the Saas-Fee road. Cross over and continue on the mule track downhill, cross a stream then traverse across the meadow with Saas-Grund immediately below. The path bends right to descend steeply, passing a chalet to reach the riverside track by the bridge. Cross the bridge to return to the centre of **Saas-Grund** (1hr 30min).

WALK 41

Saas-Grund to Saas-Fee via Bideralp

Start	Saas-Grund, 1560m
Finish	Saas-Fee, 1800m
Distance	8km
Total ascent	610m
Total descent	370m
Grade	2
Time	2hr 30min
Max altitude	1930m
Refreshments	Waldhotel Fletschhorn at Egge
Access	Post bus service between Saas-Fee and Saas-Grund

This mainly woodland walk climbs up and around the spectacular waterfalls of the Schutzbach and Biderbach gorges, visiting a number of small traditional alp settlements. First passing through the traditional village of Bidermatten, midway between Saas-Grund and Saas-Balen, the route then climbs through pine and larch woods with views of the spectacular waterfalls in the Schutzbach gorge. After crossing the torrent on a good bridge, just below the high point of the walk, the route passes the isolated chalets of Bideralp and crosses the Biderbach. It then takes in more woodland filled with alpenrose before emerging to cross an alpine meadow at Sengg, continuing on an easy track to reach the outskirts of Saas-Fee.

From the tourist office in the centre of Saas-Grund take the Saas-Fee road, cross the bridge and immediately turn right onto the gravel track on the left bank beside the Saaservispa. After 20min the track joins a small tarmac road, swinging away from the river. This soon evolves into a path as you approach **Bidermatten** across a meadow.

> **Bidermatten** (1565m) is a small traditional village lying just above the river, much of which remains unspoilt with very few recent buildings.

Walk straight through the village maintaining direction. On the far side of the little village a sign for Bideralp, Saas-Fee and the Grächen Höhenweg indicates the approaching junction where the route turns left and begins the climb.

Approaching Bidermatten across meadows

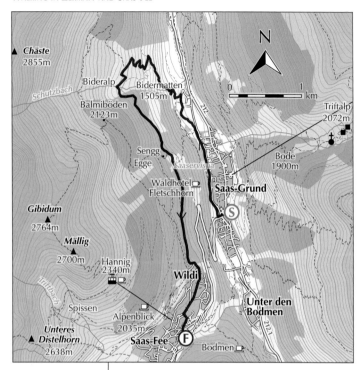

To climb to Bideralp keep on the narrow road that becomes a track and then a good path (an old mule track) and works its way up the hillside, threading through rocky outcrops at a steady gradient and constantly in the shade of larch and pine trees. After 45min from the start you will cross two torrents with elegant waterfalls and glimpses up through a rocky cleft. Continue to climb for a further 200m until you reach a path junction at a high point of 1930m. (The path to the right leads to the Grächen Höhenweg.) Continue ahead and drop briefly to cross the **Schutzbach** stream, then immediately fork right on a small path up through trees, under which bilberries and alpenrose flourish. Below is the tiny settlement

of Bideralp. Continue on the path signed 'Saas-Fee 1hr 10min, Sengg 25min'. Cross two further streams, then descend gently through woods vibrant with alpenrose in early summer.

Much of Bidermatten is still made up of old chalets and barns

Pass an isolated chalet (Brand, 1867m) in a small meadow (drinking water point), then continue through more woods. For a short while the path steepens considerably, weaving between trees and over tree roots, then the gradient eases again. At a path junction just above a small road continue straight on, climbing briefly, then emerge from the wood to cross a delightful broad alpine meadow and enter the hamlet of **Sengg** (1798m).

> **Sengg**, made up of a cluster of about a dozen traditional chalets, enjoys elevated views across the Saastal towards the alp village of Trift and the Weissmies (4017m).

To continue, follow a level path signed to Saas-Fee through yet more woods, passing the **Waldhotel Fletschhorn** (1800m) after about 15min. From here continue on a gravel track (with street lights!) gently uphill to arrive about 10min later at a track junction beside a water trough on the outskirts of Saas-Fee. To reach the centre continue to walk down the road through Wildi, and you will arrive in **Saas-Fee** in a further 5–10min.

SUMMER ALP SETTLEMENTS

Until relatively recently the inhabitants of alpine valleys such as the Mattertal and the Saastal lived as self-sufficient farming communities, growing crops, including barley, oats, rye, potatoes and summer green vegetables, and tending their animals – mainly cows, goats and chickens. Land was divided into small parcels so that everyone enjoyed high- and low-altitude land and both north- and south-facing slopes. Grain and winter feed for the animals were stored in wooden barns shared between several families, each with a precise amount of space.

Snow covers the higher alp pastures for much of the year, often beginning in October and lasting through to April or May, so cows and goats move up to the high pastures in June and July, returning to the valley in September to spend the winter indoors. This annual cycle of movement (transhumance) is accompanied by great ceremony, even today, as long processions of cows and goats, often highly decorated, follow age-old routes to and from the alp meadows. These processions begin in mid June and run through to early July in Hoferalp (Saas-Balen), Distelalp and Eyualp (Saas-Almagell), Triftalp (including traditional cow fighting) and Furggalp. A procession of goats also parades up to Hannig. Processions returning from the alp are generally held during the first week of September, when the herdsmen, who will have spent the summer in high alp settlements such as Trift, Bideralp and Hannig, return to the valleys.

Details of the precise dates each year are available from the tourist information centres and on the event calendar at www.saas-fee.ch.

WALK 42

*Saas-Grund to Triftalp, Kreuzboden
and the Weissmieshütte*

Start	Saas-Grund, 1560m
Finish	Kreuzboden, 2397m
Distance	8km
Total ascent	1200m
Total descent	330m
Grade	2
Time	4hr
Max altitude	2726m at the Weissmieshütte
Refreshments	Restaurant at Kreuzboden; Weissmieshütte; possible summer café at Triftalp
Access	Parking at the Saas-Grund gondola station. Kreuzboden is the main station on the lift
Warning	Although there are other routes to Triftalp, they are not recommended. Some maps show ascents to Triftalp through the Furwald; this is a good path through woods, but the crossing to Triftalp is closed due to rockfall. A lower crossing at 1865m, labelled 'Swisspath' and 'preachers chair', near a small chapel in Furwald is also possible, but it is steep and awkward and best avoided.

Above Saas-Grund, the Kreuzboden gondola opens up many walking opportunities in the area. Alternatively, the climb up from Saas-Grund through the hamlet of Triftalp and its attractive pastures is steep but well graded.

Sitting close under the mountains dominating the eastern wall of the Saas valley, this area is great for walking, with plenty of options in all directions. The best views are across to the peaks on the western side. The wall of mountains from the Allalinhorn and Alphubel to the Mischabel peaks (the Täschhorn, Dom, Lenzspitze and Nadelhorn) stand boldly, inaccessibly, above the Feegletscher. This, one of the Alps' finest scenes, belies the idea that these are Zermatt's mountains; clearly, they are Saas-Fee's.

The walk presents few difficulties, although there is plenty of ascent, and a variety of walking options are available: you can walk up and take the lift down or vice versa. You could also omit the hut from the walk, or simply take the gondola up and just do the Weissmieshütte section from Kreuzboden.

From the Saas-Grund gondola turn left and walk up the tarmac track for 3min through an old part of Saas-Grund to a path junction where you fork right, signed to Trift. Just before reaching a bridge over a torrent and waterfall, turn sharply right and begin to climb. This path will take you all the way to Trift in a series of zigzags. Pass a small cluster of chalets at Bode (1900m) and continue to reach

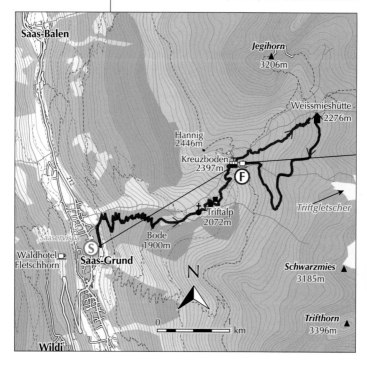

a single large chalet (former restaurant). Swing left now on a track to reach the tiny chapel and collection of chalets at **Triftalp** (2072m, 1hr).

Continue through the alp settlement to reach a junction of tracks. The path up to Kreuzboden begins just beyond the bridge.

From the path junction just east of the village, the path to Kreuzboden is clear and well signed as it climbs steadily up through pasture studded with boulders and trees, making numerous small zigzags as you gain height. ▸ After 45min cross over a track, and then cross the track a further three times to reach the **Kreuzboden gondola station** (2397m, 1hr from Trift).

The gondola station is frequently in view, always against a dramatic backdrop.

> On a sunny day and at weekends **Kreuzboden** is a popular area, and has restaurants, a children's play area, a petting zoo, go carts and scooter rental. A further gondola rises to Hohsaas at 3101m, where you can enjoy fantastic views of the snowy and glacial world of the Weissmies, Lagginhorn and neighbouring peaks. A short walk above the Hohsaas gondola station climbs past a number of special cairns, each depicting some of the major mountains in the valley, with details of their first ascents. You can walk up to Hohsaas from the Weissmieshütte, which takes 1hr 30min.

The climb to the Weissmieshütte takes 45min. The path, which essentially heads straight up, is signed by the gondola station. The hut is clearly visible ahead, and in some lights it looks black and unwelcoming. This is an illusion – as is the impression that it never seems to get any closer. Climb steeply, then continue through the next upward ramp and climb steeply again to reach the **Weissmieshütte** (2726m), which turns out to be welcoming, with wonderful views across to the Dom and the other peaks.

It is quite possible to descend to Kreuzboden using the same route, which takes around 30min – and in poor visibility this is the route to take. However, there is an

Views from Kreuzboden across to Saas-Fee and the Mischabel range

Note a mountain bike sign – you would need to be a bold mountain biker to attempt the crest of this steep moraine!

interesting alternative that is marked on the map in this guidebook, but currently not on the 'official' maps. From the hut seating area find a path heading south. It traverses and rises slightly on large slabs. After 15min you will pass under the Hohsaas gondola and descend a moraine. ◄ At a prominent cairn head left and drop down to the stream draining from the Triftgletscher (30min). Cross a small bridge and continue ahead onto a track. If you find this stream is very strong, it may be better to return to the hut and continue down the main path, as you will need to cross the stream again just above Kreuzboden.

The path now becomes an old ski track and makes one big turn before returning and emerging just above **Kreuzboden**. Recross the stream and descend to the gondola station.

From Kreuzboden, take the gondola back to **Saas-Grund gondola station**, or if you prefer to walk, you can reverse the route.

WALK 43

The Gspon Höhenweg

Start	Gspon,1893m
Finish	Kreuzboden, 2397m
Alternative finish	Saas-Grund, 1560m
Distance	14km
Total ascent	850m
Total descent	350m
Grade	3
Time	5hr
Max altitude	2470m, on the trail about 500 metres before Hannig
Refreshments	Gspon and Kreuzboden; Alp Beizli at Hoferälpji after 3hr 30min
Access	To reach the start take the bus to Stalden and cable car to Gspon; this is not covered by the Saas Citizens' Pass. Return to Saas-Grund by gondola from Kreuzboden

This is a magnificent high-level walk along the mountains facing the Mischabel peaks. Highlights of the first half of the route include views across the Rhône valley and the Balfrin and its glaciers, which are laid out for close inspection. Once you pass the halfway point, the Mischabel mountain wall comes into view.

Plenty of height is won and lost, but there are no really big climbs and few route-finding issues. Kreuzboden is signed from the start, and the walk follows Swiss Route 6 until it heads downwards at Linde Bode to Saas-Grund after 3hr (described as an alternative finish).

The middle part of the route passes a series of ravines where the mountains above are fraying somewhat, and signs give you due warning to keep moving, so there may be route changes in the future. The latter part of the route crosses rocky boulder fields, which take a little time and a lot of patience.

The route is often walked from Kreuzboden to Gspon. As there is 500m less ascent in this direction, the route takes about 30min less, and the worst rocky sections are met early on when you are fresh. On the other hand, for visitors based in the upper Saastal, walking from Gspon means you are heading 'home' and not reliant on transport at the end of the day.

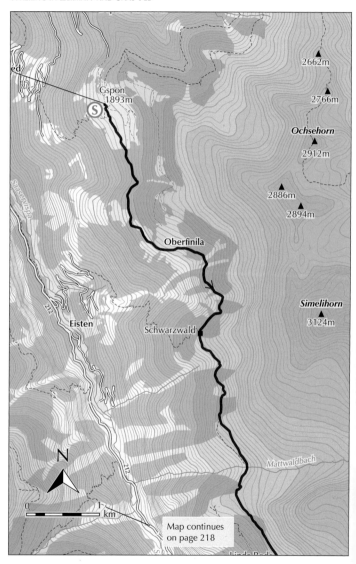

Map continues on page 218

▶ Turn right out of the cable car station and descend for a short distance on Zu Hiischina street. Kreuzboden is labelled 'Chrixbode' on the initial yellow sign. Pass through old farm buildings and walk past the sign 'Zum Wald' (the wood is just ahead). You will pass a left turn and a small shrine after 15min and a high farm after 40min. The route follows an almost level woodland trail for the first 45min, gently gaining about 100m during this time.

After 45min you will reach **Oberfinila**. Take a left turn off the track and climb to the hamlet above. Pass through chalets, then a small chapel (dated 2003), continuing to climb. ▶

Pass a left turn to Rechtung, signed 'Gspon Panoramaweg', after an hour, and 15min later climb a stone staircase then make a steep drop, the first sign of things to come. And they come soon enough, with a sign saying 'Halten Verboten/Stopping Forbidden'. With this caution in mind, cross two ravines, the second being very exposed to stonefall, to reach **Schwarzwald farm** (2191m, 1hr 40min).

Gspon is a small, sleepy ski resort that is accessed only by cable car. It offers limited winter skiing and other mid-level walks.

There is considerable ascent and descent on the trail, but most of the climbing comes in two sections: here and after Linde Bode. Most of the rest of the walk follows the continual undulation of the trail.

The Balfrin seen from the isolated farm at Schwarzwald

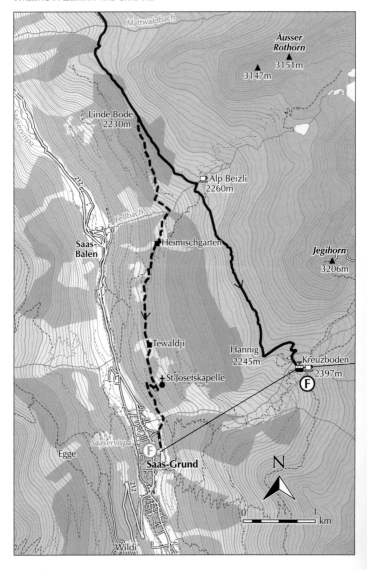

The trail climbs and descends through shaded woodland along a path that is rocky for the most part. Pass a brief cabled section and at 2hr 15min you will cross meadows with summer farm buildings. Descend to a major stream, the **Mattwaldbach**, which can be heard long before it is seen. ▸ The stream is close to the halfway point, and signs on a grassy plateau soon after indicate 2hr 30min in each direction.

The route continues in and out of woods, passing another protected section, and arrives at **Linde Bode** (2230m, 3hr), where Swiss Route 6 begins its descent to Saas-Grund (outlined below). Five minutes after this, drop to a track and turn left, and 15min later turn right signed to Hoferälpji. (The track climbs to a high tarn at Fellsee, but this is not our route.)

Soon after you will pass the only place serving refreshments on the route, the **Alp Beizli** (3hr 30min, 2260m). ▸

The onward trail climbs and passes the pastures at Grüebe, and then climbs again. At the top of a rise you will find a signpost indicating one hour to Kreuzboden. Soon after the route heads into the first of a series of boulder fields; the first is the hardest – the others have good, constructed trails. The route through the first field is obscure; keep to the right near a large boulder. You will reach **Hannig** (2445m) after 4hr 45min.

Kreuzboden is visible ahead and is reached in 15min (2397m, 5hr).

Alternative descent to Saas-Grund

The descent from Linde Bode follows Swiss Route 6 and is 6km in length; it drops 670m and takes about 2hr. At Linde Bode (2230m) take the right-hand fork in the path. As the path descends through woods, it becomes smaller and rockier, reaching the Heimischgarten restaurant (closed unfortunately) in 20min. Drop down below the former restaurant and pass between houses in the hamlet of **Heimischgarten**. Cross fields and then the substantial Fellbach stream, which cascades down to Saas-Balen. The path becomes overgrown as it descends to the pretty

The meadow before the stream would make a fine picnic site.

Drinks and cheese are available here in the high summer.

The small tarn at Kreuzboden

You can make a direct descent to Saas-Balen from the Rittmal junction.

houses at Unneri Brend. Continue along the road for 5min before the signed path reappears and drops down, crossing the road twice. ◀

Keep to the same slanting line down the hillside. Pass the house at **Tewaldji** and continue through woods on a good path. You will meet a road at a hairpin bend. Climb this for 50 metres and then take the path across meadows to Bodme, another very attractive hamlet with narrow pathways between the houses.

After Bodme keep to a narrow path just above the road and drop to the **St Josefskapelle**, which has fine views of Saas-Grund. At a road, cross through a curious gap in the protective mesh and drop down through the old village of Unter dem Berg before reaching the bottom of the **Kreuzboden** lift (1560m, 5hr).

WALK 44

The descent of the Saastal –
Mattmark to Saas-Balen

Start	Mattmark Dam, 2204m
Finish	Saas-Balen, 1483m
Alternative finish	Saas-Almagell, 1670m, or Saas-Grund, 1560m
Distance	16km
Total ascent	170m
Total descent	890m
Grade	1–2
Time	4hr–4hr 30min
Max altitude	2204m at Mattmark
Refreshments	Mattmark, Saas-Almagell, Unter den Bodmen, Saas-Grund, Saas-Balen
Access	A regular bus service serves the entire route
Note	This route can be split easily into shorter sections using the regular postbus service.
Warning	The initial steep path from Mattmark has suffered from some recent small landslides, and the path may be re-routed slightly in the future.

This almost entirely downhill walk explores the valley of the Saaservispa river and the Saastal between the Mattmark and Saas-Balen. The nature of the path is varied; the initial descent path from the lake is steep and slightly exposed (giving this walk a Grade 2 element), but this can be avoided by following an optional track. The remaining sections of the route are a delightful mix of larch woodland, riverside walking and a beautiful section of path between Saas-Almagell and Unter den Bodmen, which has all the elements of a mini alpine adventure, crossing a spectacular waterfall, following a leat and encountering a few minor rock and boulder sections.

If you plan to walk the entire route in the opposite direction, allow an extra 1hr 30min.

From the Mattmark restaurant and bus stop walk to the far end of the dam wall (north-east side of the lake), then

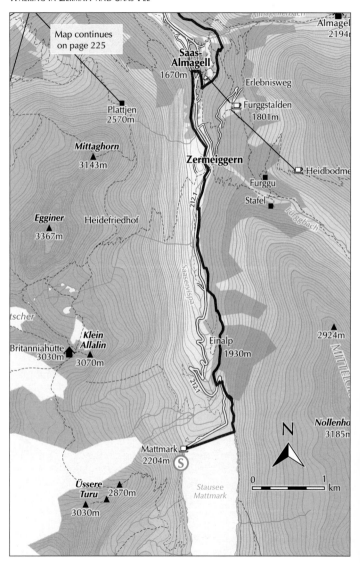

Map continues
on page 225

Almagel
2194m

Saas-
Almagell
1670m

Erlebnisweg

Furggstalden
1801m

Plattjen
2570m

Mittaghorn
3143m

Zermeiggern

Heidbodme

Furggu

Stafel

Egginer
3367m

Heidefriedhof

2924m

*Klein
Allalin*
3070m

Britanniahütte
3030m

Einalp
1930m

Nollenho
3185m

N

Mattmark
2204m
S

0   1
km

*Üssere
Turu*
3030m   2870m

Stausee
Mattmark

222

take the track north and descend easily for 3min. At the point where the track makes a hairpin bend, continue ahead on a small path that drops fairly steeply down the hillside in a series of tight zigzags, before traversing the hillside and dropping again to the road. Cross the road twice then descend gently on a broad grassy track. At a hairpin in the track continue on the path straight ahead, traversing the hillside towards a group of chalets at **Eienalp** (1930m).

From here follow the signs and continue down through woods on occasional short steeper sections, then pass through a large stretch of old boulder field. The path now descends to the road next to a perfect small pool and picnic area. Cross the road and walk on the broad grass verge, then cross the bridge and continue past the electricity substation. Just before the next bridge take the track to the left to reach **Saas-Almagell** (6km, 1670m, 1hr 40min).

> The **next section** between Saas-Almagell and Unter den Bodmen is a delightful route suitable for families, although children should be old enough to understand the dangers of mildly exposed situations. The sign at the beginning of the route suggests the route can be walked in 1hr 40min.

Cross the bridge to enter the village, then turn right and walk up to the Furggstalden chairlift station. Locate a path to the left of the building, signed '1hr 40min to Saas-Grund', which rises gently in a northerly direction next to a leat. Climb through larch woods next to the leat for about 10min to reach a path junction where you continue straight ahead, signed to Zum Moss, Saas-Grund and Saas-Balen. After two sharp turns in the path as it climbs, the gradient eases and it crosses one or two small streams before arriving at a metal bridge that spans the **Almagellerbach** as it plummets in a spectacular cascade.

Cross the bridge and continue straight on, ignoring the paths either side, and enter another larch wood,

The path is incredibly pretty and easy underfoot.

now following another leat as it gently descends. ◄ It now threads its way through a boulder field, but without difficulty, save for two short sections where one or two steep steps are protected with a cable. The path now briefly steepens downhill, with an optional path to Zum Moss. After 1hr 20min from Saas-Almagell turn left and descend to level off just above the road, where there is a large welcome sign for a campsite at **Unter den Bodmen**.

Enter the village through the campsite then turn right to continue north through the village past another camp site, then cross to the left bank of the river and continue on the track, passing another campsite before arriving at **Saas-Grund** (6km, 1560m, 1hr 45min from Saas-Almagell). Keeping to the left bank of the river, walk down the track towards Bidermatten and pass directly through the small village. ◄ At the far side of **Bidermatten** take the small, signed road ahead and slightly uphill. Pass through a small parking area and onto a track that continues across meadows. Soon the cascading waterfalls of the Schutzbach come into view to the left, with a bridge crossing the lower section of the torrent. Shortly, the road becomes a track that begins a long gentle descent through larch woods. Just after passing a large builder's yard, seen through the trees below, join the riverside track by a large boulder and almost immediately fork left onto a path that leads directly towards the round church of **Saas-Balen** (1483m, 1hr from Saas-Grund). The bus stop is just the other side of the bridge.

Although a riverside walk from here to Saas-Balen is possible, the recommended route stays higher above the river, crossing a meadow with views of waterfalls and descending through larch woods.

> **Saas-Balen** is the least developed of the Saas villages as a tourist destination; however, it does have a restaurant and a shop. The church of Saas-Balen is unusual – it is entirely round! It's worth taking a few minutes to look inside. The chapel was constructed between 1710 and 1712 on the same site as an earlier building dating from the 16th and 17th centuries. Much of the internal decoration dates from the 19th century, while the gothic main altar, carved locally, dates from 1764.

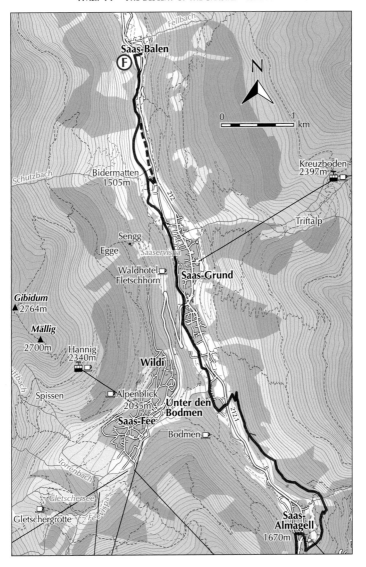

The round church at Saas-Balen

WALK 45

Almagelleralp and the Almagellerhütte

Start/finish	Saas-Almagell (1672m)
Distance	15km
Total ascent/descent	1230m
Grade	3
Time	6hr
Max altitude	2894m at the Almagellerhütte
Refreshments	Saas-Almagell, Berghotel Almagelleralp, Almagellerhütte
Access	Public transport to Saas-Almagell; parking in the village

This high mountain walk takes in a well-known mountain inn at Almagelleralp and a high mountain hut. After a steep climb above the village, the Almagellertal becomes a most attractive hanging valley: narrow before the *berghotel* and widening as the upper valley is reached. The climb to the Almagellerhütte is straightforward on good paths that face south, which means they lose snow early in the summer. The views back to the Mischabel peaks from many points of the route match any in the Alps.

Although the ascent route can be reversed, other descent routes are recommended. An alternative route to Almagelleralp is the Erlebnisweg, a via-ferrata-like route via Furggstalden, which is described in Walk 46.

In the event of bad weather, or if you feel the need for a shorter day, the route can be shortened by not making the climb to the Almagellerhütte. This would leave a route of about 8km, which would take 3hr 30min, allowing ample time for a long lunch in the Berghotel Almagelleralp.

From the central square in Saas-Almagell, walk 5min south to the bottom station of the chairlift to Furggstalden. Take the rising path on the left alongside the water channel. ▸

After 15min take a right turn and then turn left after another 5min. The way ahead is now clear, and the

If starting from the centre of the village, pass between houses and climb to join this path.

Sheep grazing high in the Almagellertal

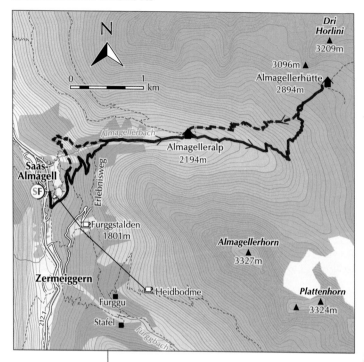

path climbs steadily in zigzags through the woods, with glimpses down to Saas-Almagell and increasing views across to the mountains above Saas-Fee.

After an hour (at 2020m) you will meet a path joining on the right from Furggstalden, which follows the via-ferrata-like Erlebnisweg (also known as the Almagell Adventure Trail). This has bridges, cables, stemples, walkways and ladders, but requires no special equipment – just a head for heights. Turn left and 5min later cross a wooden bridge and turn right to climb steadily into the Almagellertal alongside the Almagellerbach stream for 30min. The trail is not steep but eventually flattens, and the **Berghotel Almagelleralp** is seen and soon reached (2194m, 1hr 45min).

A night in the **Berghotel Almagelleralp** (or the higher refuge) is easy to organise and a good place to start your mountain hut experience. The inn has private rooms. The sunset and sunrise from both huts, as well as the views across the valley and their remote locations, make these experiences to savour. Notes on what to expect when staying in a mountain hut are included in the main Introduction, and contact details are given in the introduction to this chapter.

From Almagelleralp it takes 1hr 45min to reach the Almagellerhütte. Head straight up the valley on a good path. Avoid small trails heading directly up the valley after 30min (2370m), and after 1hr (2560m) pass a prominent board advertising the hut. ▸

After 1hr 30min a path joins from the left. This will be the descent route.

The hut is now in sight. Continue straight ahead to reach the beautifully sited **Almagellerhütte** (2894m, 3hr 30min).

You can descend to the Almagelleralp by reversing the ascent path, but if you prefer a different route, take the path to the right 10min after leaving the hut. There are no route-finding distractions, but this path is noticeably smaller and rougher than the ascent path. Descend with care and come out above **Almagelleralp** before joining

The Almagellerhütte

another path; the *berghotel* is 3min to the left (1hr 15min from the hut, 4hr 45min from the start).

Again, to reach Saas-Almagell the ascent route can be reversed, but a descent by the Almagellerbach waterfall, which takes 1hr 15min, is recommended.

Descend to the bridge but do not cross it, then continue down on the true right bank of the **Almagellerbach**. After 500 metres, the path turns away from the stream onto rockier, steeper ground, then narrows and drops quickly. Meet a path from Saas-Grund and turn left. The path crosses the stream on a solid metal bridge, close under the waterfall but still keeping dry, before dropping back to **Saas-Almagell** (1670m, 6hr) either direct to the centre or to the bottom chairlift station.

WALK 46

The höhenweg from Saas-Almagell to Kreuzboden

Start	Saas-Almagell, 1672m
Finish	Kreuzboden, 2397m
Distance	13km
Total ascent	900m
Total descent	170m
Grade	3 (with a short but avoidable Grade 4 passage on the Erlebnisweg)
Time	5hr
Max altitude	2530m
Refreshments	Saas-Almagell, Almagelleralp, Kreuzboden
Access	Descend by gondola from Kreuzboden to Saas-Grund. Optional chairlift from Saas-Almagell to Furggstalden
Warning	This route involves ladders, metal steps and exposed steep paths, as well as two rope suspension bridges. At all times the path is well protected with cables and other aids; however, if you are uncomfortable in highly exposed situations, this might not be the best route for you. Experienced walkers who are familiar with this type of high-level path with aided sections will have great fun.

This is an exciting outing, with a via-ferrata-like challenge at the start and a great high mountain traverse to follow. Although the actual walking time from Saas-Almagell to the Almagelleralp via the Erlebnisweg is signed as 1hr 30min, parties should realistically allow at least 2hr–2hr 30min for the first part of the route. If you don't fancy the Erlebnisweg, take the ascent route described in Walk 45 and join the walk at the Almagellerbach stream, which will save you at least 30min.

The *höhenweg* from idyllic Almagelleralp to Kreuzboden is full of interest and superb, uninterrupted views. The path is good and although exposed in some places, the constant feeling of excitement you have is more to do with the fantastic views. You will find you stop to take a great many photographs!

Begin at the Furggstalden chairlift station 5min south of the centre of Saas-Almagell and take the path just to the left, which climbs next to a fast-flowing leat. Climb gently, taking the right fork signed to Almagelleralp. The path heads north, then switches south as it climbs. At the next path junction continue straight ahead still in a southerly

Good protection on the Erlebnisweg

231

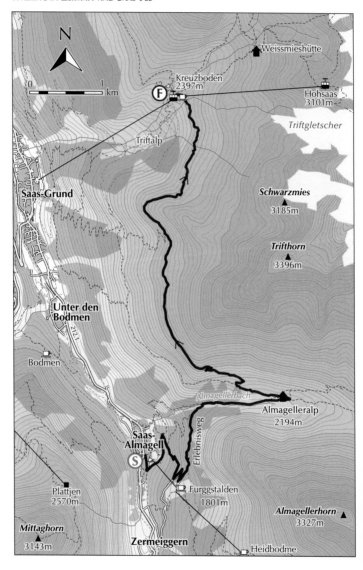

direction and continue to climb fairly steeply but steadily. After about 1hr 15min the path levels out to eventually meet a small road with a sign to Restaurant Alpina.
Turn left and walk up the road and round two hairpin
bends to reach a small parking area at **Furggstalden**. The
path for the Erlebnisweg, which is clearly signed, continues straight ahead. Alternatively, take the chairlift to
Furggstalden, then walk up the road to the parking area
and join the route.

Leave the road and within 2–3min you will begin the
Erlebnisweg. Climb a sturdy metal ladder, almost a staircase, followed by a flight of metal steps set into the rock.
Continue to climb, seemingly vertically, on more ladders
and steps, always with good protection and a cable to
hold onto. The route levels out through a short wooded
section before meeting the first of two rope bridges. ▶

Immediately after crossing the bridge, the path plummets down a steep flight of metal steps attached to a rock,
then continues to traverse the hillside before climbing to
the second bridge. After this, the path becomes easier,
climbing gently through woods to meet the main path
from Saas-Almagell. At the path junction turn right, cross
the **Almagellerbach**, and continue up the delightful valley for 30min to the **Berghotel Almagelleralp** (2194m,
1hr 30min–2hr).

From here the *höhenweg* path to Kreuzboden takes
2hr 30min–3hr. Starting at the west side of the refuge,
clearly marked with a red-and-white paint splash, walk
up the path and after 50 metres take the right fork signed
'Obere Blattebode, Chrizbode and Höhenweg'. Climb
gently, traversing a gentle grassy hillside dotted with
boulders and full of flowers in early summer. After 20min
you will reach a path junction, with the *höhenweg* signed
to the right. Continue to climb, traversing the hillside, at
times a little more steeply.

Views to the south and the Mattmark are revealed,
while the views back up the **Almagellertal valley** are
of snow and ice and of a prominent moraine left by

Only three people
should be on the
bridge at the same
time, and do not
attempt to cross while
anyone is coming
the other way.

The höhenweg path traverses the mountains above the Saas valley

the Rotblatt glacier, the peaks of the Almagellerhorn and Portjengrat dominating the skyline.

The path now climbs more steeply in a short series of zigzags to round the corner and leave the Almagellertal (2300m, 1hr).

The route climbs more gently now and after a further 15min you will reach a higher point at 2394m. ◀ The path now drops 30m to pass beneath a huge area of rock slabs, then climbs again to cross a large boulder field. Pass through a small iron gate and continue on a mostly rocky path, then climb gently to traverse a grassy slope (2500m, 1hr 45min from Almagelleralp).

Here there are superb views out across the main valley to the Mischabel range above Saas-Fee.

The entire **Kreuzboden–Almagelleralp Höhenweg** enjoys superb views of the Saas valley, with Saas-Fee and the Mischabel range dominating throughout, and the distant Mattmark and Monte Moro Pass in the far distance to the south. The route is almost entirely above the treeline. In summer the path and hillsides are filled with flowers, and the route is always interesting.

Looking across a huge grassy bowl, you will see the hillside ahead is covered with sturdy avalanche defences. The path leads across a large flat area with a wooden hut used for avalanche defence equipment. It then descends on a track, resuming on a path straight ahead (signed '1hr 15min to Kreuzboden') at a hairpin bend. Climb up through the avalanche area, skirting round the rocky bluff with cables to assist. You will arrive, 2hr 45min from Almagelleralp, at a high point as the Trift valley comes into view.

The path now crosses through a vast area of boulders, but the way is well marked and the path through the boulders is obvious. In early summer some snow patches may remain, requiring care when crossing. With the boulder field finally behind you, a good path eases down the remaining hillside, crossing over the cascading Triftbach just before reaching the **Kreuzboden gondola station** (2397m, 5hr from Saas-Almagell).

WALK 47
Furggstalden and the Furggtälli

Start/finish	Saas-Almagell, 1672m
Distance	12km
Total ascent/descent	700m
Grade	2
Time	4hr
Max altitude	2302m at the bridge in the Furggtälli
Refreshments	Restaurants at Furggstalden
Access	Optional chairlift from Saas-Almagell to Furggstalden

This is a walk for enjoying the solitude and rugged beauty of the long Furggtälli valley, at the head of which is the Antronapass. The cluster of houses and two restaurants at Furggstalden can be reached by following either the ascent or descent paths described below or by taking the chairlift from Saas-Almagell. The route passes through pine and larch woods as it approaches the entrance to the valley. Soon the trees become sparse, and the walk continues through an exquisite natural rock garden with juniper, alpenrose and every imaginable variety of alpine flower before it stretches up into the raw beauty and solitude of the higher reaches of the valley.

It is also possible to walk to a high lift station and café at Heidbodme, which takes 2hr (there and back), or you can use the chairlift up from Furggstalden. There are great views across to Monte Rosa from Heidbodme.

From the square in the centre of Saas-Almagell, head south to the *talstation*. Here, turn left and take the contouring path above Saas-Almagell. ◄ In less than 100 metres, find a right turn and take this path, which climbs directly uphill. Climb for 30min, cross a track and continue straight on through the hamlet of **Furggstalden** (1801m) and emerge onto more open ground. To the right is the top chairlift station, ahead are two restaurants and on the left is the track to the Furggtälli, signed 'Antronapass' – take this path. (An easier climb through woods – but only a little easier – can be made by not taking the steep track at the bottom but by continuing and taking the next main turn right; this is described in Walk 45.) Alternatively, take the chairlift up to Furggstalden.

This is a leat path and the water runs gently alongside.

Take the left-hand turn and climb up the small road, signed to the Antronapass. Pass a small car park after which the road then becomes a track as it doubles back and continues a gradual ascent above Furggstalden. A path joins from the right; this is a direct route from Furggstalden, but it is tricky to find from the other end. The track dwindles into a path and continues to reach the farm of **Furggu**, 45min after leaving the top station. ◄

Views into the valley and up towards the Antronapass on the Italian border show a wild and unspoilt glen.

From the Furggu chalets continue ahead to enter the Furggtälli valley, keeping the stream to your right. This first section of the valley is lightly wooded and gently climbs through the most exquisite natural rock garden, with juniper and alpenrose in late June and July, as well as every imaginable alpine flower vying for your attention. Cross a side stream and as you enter the middle

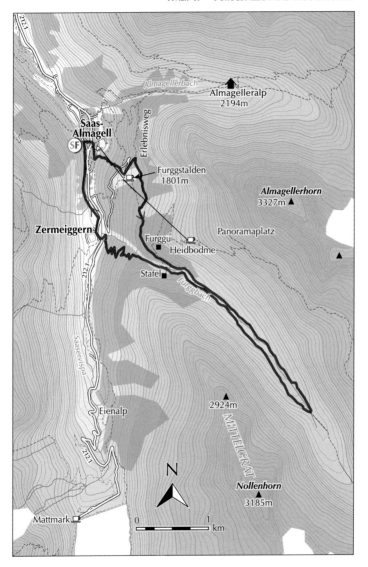

237

*The view along
the Furggtälli to
the Antronapass*

section of the valley, the path continues to rise very
gently.

> The **Furggtälli** is a wild and very beautiful place but
> seldom visited, as it sits above the treeline and there
> are no restaurants or other evidence of develop-
> ment. The Antronapass is constantly in view at the
> head of the valley, the paths and the stream cradled
> between the slopes on either side.

After climbing onto a moraine, a well-made section
of stone path climbs through boulders to reach the crossing point at a small concrete outflow. The path ahead
goes directly to the Antronapass; however, this walk turns
right and proceeds down the path on the other side of the
stream (1hr from Furggu).

The walk back down is very pleasant, on a slightly
rougher path at times, and in just under an hour you
reach the isolated **Stafel** chalet. Just beyond the chalet
a path is signed 'Zermeiggern 35min'. This path makes a
series of zigzags at a good gradient all the way to the valley road to emerge at a bridge near **Zermeiggern**.

To return to Saas-Almagell, turn right and either walk down beside the road or walk beside the road for 3min and then take a track forking left just before a bridge. Both will lead directly back to **Saas-Almagell** within 15–20min.

WALK 48
Schwarzbergalp and circuit of the Mattmark

Start/finish	Mattmark dam wall at the restaurant, 2204m
Distance	12km (8km for Mattmark circuit only)
Total ascent/descent	590m (80m for Mattmark circuit only)
Grade	3 (1 for the Mattmark circuit only)
Time	4hr 30min (2hr 15min for Mattmark circuit only)
Max altitude	2693m
Refreshments	Restaurant Mattmark
Access	Postbus from the Saas valley
Note	This walk is essentially a walk of two halves; the ascent to the Schwarzbergalp viewpoint is on a good path, but it is an airy and steep high mountain path requiring a good level of fitness – quite different from the almost flat, wide track that circumnavigates the lake. The Grade 3 is indicative of this ascent, while a simple circuit of Mattmark warrants a Grade 1.

The first part of the walk is a climb to a superb viewpoint amid a world of snow and ice, with excellent views of the frontier peaks rimming the Schwarzberggletscher, less than 4km away. A good path follows the crest of a lateral moraine for much of the way, before it climbs more steeply up the final 200 metres to reach the high point.

The circumnavigation of the Mattmark is suitable for all walkers who are able to complete the distance, presenting few or no navigation difficulties. In early summer the hillsides are covered in an abundance of flowering alpenrose, which contrasts with the many meltwater cascades as they plummet towards the lake below. The views towards Monte Moro (2985m) and the Monte Moro Pass (Walk 49) are excellent.

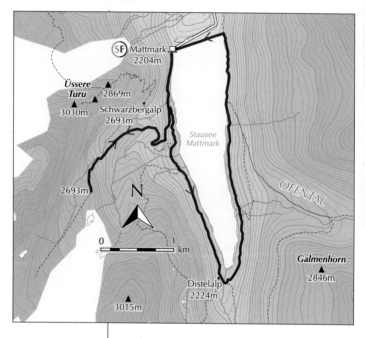

From the dam wall of the Mattmark, walk past the restaurant and begin the walk along the west side of the reservoir. After a 5min walk through a well-lit tunnel (no headtorch required), cross a bridge with a huge cascade of water coming from above. About 10min after the start the track forks, with a rising right-hand track signed to 'Schwarzbärg, Schwarzbärggletscher'.

Take the right-hand fork and walk up the track for 10min, keeping right on the track where a blue signpost signals a path to the left. Continue up the track for a further 5min.

At a second junction, turn left on a red/white signed path, which rises steadily up the side of the moraine. At 2366m the path diverges beside a large boulder. Both paths meet at a point higher up; the left path runs along the crest of the larger moraine, with tremendous views

across a landscape of bare rock scoured by the retreating Schwarzberggletscher, while the right-hand path is less exposed, and for the main part follows a lower, grassier path.

Shortly after the paths reunite, at 2513m, leave the crest of the moraine and drop slightly to the right, but always staying to the left of a stream. The clear path now steepens considerably, climbing more moraine to reach the high point at **2693m**, marked by a cairn, about one hour from the turn on the track below.

The views from the high point down onto the **Schwarzberggletscher** are sublime. This is a world of snow and ice, crowned by the frontier peaks of the Schwarzberghorn (3609m) and the Steinchalchhorn (3333m). Enjoy the view and linger a while – you will almost certainly have the entire valley to yourself.

To descend, simply retrace your route, then either turn left at the main Mattmark circuit track to return to the restaurant and postbus service or turn right to walk around the lake.

The moraine ascent from Schwarzbergalp

Looking back towards the dam from the head of the Mattmark

The circuit of the Mattmark

The route on the west side of the lake follows a roughly level, mainly tarmacked track that leads to the head of the lake at **Distelalp** (2224m). Here there are signs for the Monte Moro Pass ahead.

> The **Monte Moro Pass** is visible ahead. The Monte Moro peak can be seen slightly to the right of the pass and the Joderhorn to the left. On a clear day it's even possible to make out the golden statue of the Madonna set slightly to the west above the pass.

Cross the bridge and begin the return walk, this time on a rougher track that rises slightly, using small bridges to cross a series of torrents that feed the lake. ◄ Finally, descend to the level of the top of the dam, turn left and walk along the dam wall back to the **Mattmark restaurant** and bus stop.

In late June and July these hillsides are painted red with alpenrose.

THE MATTMARK DAM

Memorial plaque to the workers who died while building the Mattmark dam

The idea for the dam originated early in the 20th century; however, the dam was built between 1960 and 1965, and later extended. On 30 August 1965 a large avalanche from the Allalingletscher (which can be seen to the west above the dam wall) destroyed the cabins housing the construction workers and 88 people were killed.

The dam wall is made of earth and covered in rocks, and it is Europe's largest earthen dam. Power is generated in Stalden and Saas-Almagell, with an annual production of 665GWh. The small reservoir at Zermeiggern, just above Saas-Almagell, pumps water upwards for recirculation at times of low demand. On the path across the dam wall at the end of the route, a series of plaques explain the history of the valley and the dam.

WALK 49

The Monte Moro Pass

Start/finish	Mattmark, 2204m
Distance	15km
Total ascent/descent	720m
Grade	3
Time	5hr
Max altitude	2853m at the Monte Moro Pass; 2870m at the Madonna statue
Refreshments	Mattmark restaurant at the start/finish. The Rifugio Monte Moro (also known as Rifugio Oberto Maroli) is 50m below the col in Italy
Access	Bus to Mattmark (parking)
Note	Take your passport if you plan to drop down into Italy, just in case.

Topped by a golden Madonna, the Monte Moro Pass has been a trade passage for many centuries, and is the gateway to Italy. The Tour of Monte Rosa, one of the finest long-distance hikes in the Alps, crosses the pass on its route to Macugnaga. The pass looks west to the stunning east face of Monte Rosa and has a welcoming refuge just below on the Italian side. Cable cars ascend from Macugnaga, and on a sunny weekend the pass is a popular spot with Italian visitors.

The route is straightforward until it reaches Tälliboden, from where it climbs more steeply over rocky ledges and ramps with occasional protection. It is a high route with fine views, so tackle it on a fine, settled day, making a note of the last bus back from the Mattmark.

An alternative descent can be made through the Ofental valley from Tälliboden, which would add an extra 200m of height gain and loss and an additional hour.

From the Mattmark restaurant and bus stop, walk to the corner of the dam wall and follow the western shore on a track heading south. After 5min take the left-hand tunnel. Pass the turn to Schwarzbergalp after 10min and after 15min pass to the left of another tunnel. ◀ Cross two streams on the western shore; you will see others nearly 1km away across the Mattmark.

Large streams collect the glacial melt in summer and crash noisily into the reservoir.

The tarmacked track leads directly to the far end of the reservoir (**Distelalp**, 2224m), where you will arrive in under an hour. From here the golden Madonna statue above the col can be spotted on a clear day.

Just after crossing the stream that feeds into the reservoir, turn right and begin the climb. The path climbs steadily through the valley. In places there are two options you can take but all arrive at **Tälliboden** (2492m, 1hr 45min), 50min from the end of the reservoir.

The path to the Monte Moro Pass turns right across grassy pasture then swings left to begin the climb directly towards the pass up the rocky hillside in a series of ramps and ledges. The path is well engineered, with rocky steps linking large rock slabs. The way is clearly marked with paint splashes and occasional small cairns; however, in early summer large patches of snow may cover much of

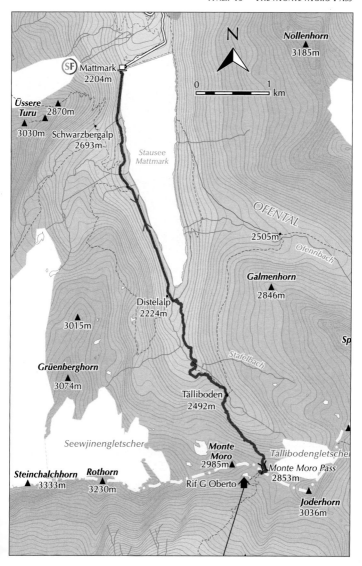

Steps on the climb to the Monte Moro Pass

this signage. Even in late summer you may need to cross short sections of snow, but these shouldn't present any difficulty.

The final 50m of ascent is slightly rockier and more difficult before you reach the **Monte Moro Pass** (2853m), 3hr after leaving the Mattmark dam. The short climb to the golden Madonna involves using a few metal steps set into the rock, with cables, from where the views across to the Monte Rosa and in all other directions are superb.

THE MONTE MORO PASS (2853M)

The Monte Moro Pass has been a trade route for many centuries. In the 14th century the Walser people migrated across to Macugnaga and the Domodossola valley in northern Italy. The pass is capped by a 5m-high golden statue of la Madonna della Neve (Madonna of the Snow).

Rifugio Oberto Maroli is located about 40–50m (10min) below the statue, next to a small lake and the cable car to Macugnaga.

To return to Mattmark, retrace the route to Tälliboden and Distelalp. For variety, if for no other reason, take the eastern side of the dam, which takes 15min longer than the western side, and return to **Mattmark**. ▶

Plaques along the dam wall path tell the story of the dam and its construction.

WALK 50
The Ofental, Jazzilücke and Antronapass

Start	Mattmark, 2204m
Finish	Heidbodme, 2346m
Alternative finish	Saas-Almagell, 1670m
Distance	18km (alternative 22km)
Total ascent	1090m (alternative 1090m)
Total descent	950m (alternative 1620m)
Grade	3 with a short section of 4 between the Jazzilücke and Antronapass
Time	6hr 45min
Max altitude	3081m at the Jazzilücke
Refreshments	Mattmark restaurant at the start, Heidbodme gondola station at the finish, Furggstalden
Access	Valley bus to Mattmark; gondola descent from Heidbodme and Furggstalden
Warning	Check conditions first, as snow or bad weather would turn this route into a serious undertaking. Be aware of transport times.

The Jazzilücke–Antronapass traverse is a fine and committing day-long walk, one of the best in the Saastal. Climbing above the Mattmark, the route enters the remote and peaceful Ofental valley and climbs to the Jazzilücke col at 3081m, before making a short high traverse and descending to the Antronapass. A new high-level route continues to Heidbodme and a well-earned gondola down. It is a challenging day, with views towards the Saas peaks and down into Italy's Antronapass valley.

Timing is important. The first bus to Mattmark arrives just before 0830 and the last lift down from Heidbodme is at 1630, so there isn't time to dawdle. Check bus and lift times before setting off and keep an eye on the clock, especially at Antronapass, where a descent through the Fürggtalli valley is a possibility.

The crux of the route is an hour-long section between the Jazzilücke and the Antronapass, and particularly the first 15min of this section. The route makes a traverse at nearly 3100m and is undoubtedly exposed but also well protected by cables on a good path. The Swiss authorities have classified it as a red *bergwanderweg* rather than a blue alpine route, which is a close call; however, this section is at most 400 metres long. The descent of a broad ridge to the Antronapass is more straightforward. Under snow, this east-facing crux section would represent a significant mountaineering expedition so check conditions first.

Cross the Mattmark dam wall and turn right along the shore of the lake. After 25min turn left on a small path that climbs above the lake onto a broad terrace. After climbing 200m the path levels and passes through broad pastures of grazing cows and sheep. At **2505m** you will come to a path junction (1hr 20min).

Take the left-hand path and continue steadily up the valley. After 5min you will pass through a flat area where the Ofentalbach stream splits into braids. Continue upwards in the wide, quiet valley. At a path junction at **2721m** (2hr) turn left for the climb to the col. The path is marked by waymarks, poles and occasional cairns but

Cattle grazing in the Ofental valley

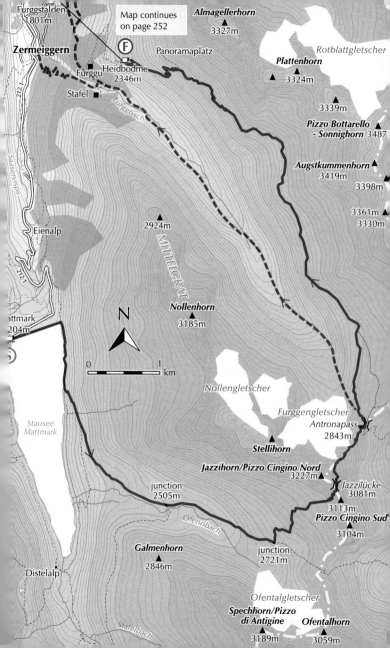

Furggstalden
1.801m

Zermeiggern

Map continues
on page 252

(F)

Panoramaplatz

Fürggu

Heidbodme
2346m

Stafel

Almagellerhorn
3327m

Rotblattgletscher

Plattenhorn
△ 3324m

3339m

*Pizzo Bottarello
- Sonnighorn* 3487

Augstkummenhorn
3419m
△ 3398m

3361m
3330m

Furggbach

Saaservispa

Eienalp

2924m

MITTELGRAT

Nollenhorn
3185m

N

0   1

km

attmark
204m

Nollengletscher

Furggengletscher

Antronapass
2843m

Stausee
Mattmark

Stellihorn

Jazzihorn/Pizzo Cingino Nord
3227m

Jazzilücke
3081m

3113m

Pizzo Cingino Sud
3104m

junction
2505m

Ofennbach

Galmenhorn
2846m

junction
2721m

Distelalp

Ofentalgletscher

Statelbach

*Spechhorn/Pizzo
di Antigine*
3189m

Ofentalhorn
3059m

early in the climb it crosses level stones so care is needed to stay on course. After passing a large boulder, the path steepens and climbs the final 200m to the **Jazzilücke** (3081m, 3hr).

After the steep but reasonable climb, the change is dramatic. The onward path is tucked into the vertical cliffs of the Jazzihorn. It looks almost impossible, with vast drop-offs to the east and a serious level of exposure, but be reassured, a good path protected by strong cable makes its way across the mountainside. The challenging section takes 45–60min: about 15min crossing the cliffs and about 45min descending the ridge to the Antronapass. If you change your mind now that you have seen what you have in store, the Jazzilücke is the place to turn around. ◄

Far below, in Italy, the Lago di Cingino glistens attractively with an unmanned refuge on its shores.

The initial 25 metres have no cable but soon pick one up – this is almost continuous until you have passed the main difficulties. After the cabled section there are likely to be snow patches, some of which may last all year. Emerge at the start of a broad ridge dropping to the north-east.

The ridge narrows as you descend. As far as possible, stay on the ridge, although the path passes under a rock on the north side, and lower down the best routes are on the southern/Italian side. The best line is clearly waymarked. Arrive at the **Antronapass** (2843m, 4hr).

> The **Antronapass** (Passo di Saas in Italian) has been used as a trade route between Switzerland and Italy since the 13th century. The remains of a salt store at the pass date from 1792.

Here take stock of the time. The last mid-summer gondola from Heidbodme leaves at 1630 (but check in advance). The high traverse above the Furggtälli is a long route and the signed time of 2hr 30min is quite a stern test; a more realistic time is 2hr 45min–3hr. The distance is 8.5km with 200m of ascent and 700m of descent, but nearer Heidbodme the route crosses rocks and slabs, so progress is slower. If you think you might miss the last lift, consider taking the route through the Furggtälli valley instead (outlined below).

Both the high-level route to Heidbodme and the alternative route through the Furggtälli descend directly from the col. (An older route heads up from the col; this is now disused.) After 5min, turn right signed to Heidbodme. The path crosses level stones for 30min and is well marked but take care; keeping to the path would be challenging if thick cloud came in.

Contour around a bowl on the vast hillside. The route climbs towards a rock outcrop, somewhat unexpectedly on steps and with chains, arriving at a sign announcing you are at Beerterrigg (2800m, 5hr 10min). Continue, now on easier ground and pass a sign at Oügschtchumme (2730m, 5hr 35min) to reach a second steep climb through rocks, again supported by cables and steps (2750m, 6hr).

Now pass through an area of vast rock slabs. The path is well made but inevitably water and rock fall will disrupt this part of the route, and progress will be slower.

The high path along the Furggtälli to Heidbodme

251

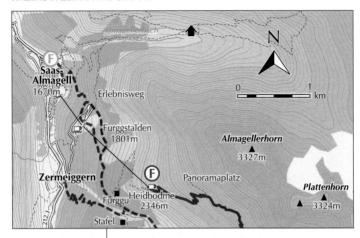

Pass a sign for 'Panoramaplatz' (6hr 20min) and start to descend to the small gondola station now visible below, arriving at **Heidbodme** (2346m, 6hr 45min).

From Heidbodme take the small lift down then walk 10min to the Furggstalden chairlift. Take this or walk past the chairlift and take the steep descent path to **Saas-Almagell**. If you miss the last lift from Heidbodme, the walk down will take about 1hr 45min. Follow the path from Heidbodme to Furggstalden and then the steep descent through woods to Saas-Almagell (1672m, 8hr 30min).

Alternative descent from Antronapass by Fürggtalli valley

If you decide not to do the high-level route to Heidbodme, continue straight down the valley. The initial part of the descent is long and over rocky ground before the path levels out below 2400m and becomes a greener and very pleasant, if long, walk. To reach the valley, head to **Stafel** to descend to the Zermeiggern and walk down paths alongside the road to Saas-Almagell. Alternatively, keep right to Furggu and descend to reach **Furggstalden** and then descend steeply through woods directly to **Saas-Almagell** (4hr).

APPENDIX A
Useful contacts

Local tourist offices
Zermatt
Bahnhofplatz 5
3920 Zermatt
tel +41 27 966 81 00
www.zermatt.ch
(also offices in Täsch and Randa)

Grächen and St Niklaus
Dorfplatz
3925 Grächen
tel +41 27 955 60 60
www.graechen.ch

Saas-Fee
3906 Saas-Fee
tel +41 27 958 18 58
www.saas-fee.ch
(also offices in Saas-Grund and
Saas-Almagell)

Tourist information
Switzerland Tourism (UK)
tel 00800 100 200 29 (free)
email info.uk@myswitzerland.com
www.myswitzerland.com

Swiss National Tourist Office (USA)
tel (212) 757 5944
email info.usa@myswitzerland.com

Swiss Tourism (Australia)
tel +61 2 8866 3420

Swiss Alpine Club
www.sac-cas.ch/en

Swiss Hiking Trail Federation
www.schweizmobil.ch

Map suppliers
Stanfords
tel 0207 836 1321
email sales@stanfords.co.uk
www.stanfords.co.uk

The Map Shop
tel 01684 593146
0800 085 40 80 (UK only)
email themapshop@btinternet.com
www.themapshop.co.uk

Swisstopo
www.map.geo.admin.ch

USA
Omnimap.com

Apps
Meteoswiss – Swiss weather forecasting

SBB Mobile – all Swiss public transport

OUI.sncf – French rail booking

Swiss Map – Swisstopo mapping to buy
and download

Phonemaps – open data mapping with
footpaths

ViewRanger – mapping and routes.
Open data maps, with options to
purchase Swisstopo maps

Mountain huts and restaurants

Zermatt
Bergrestaurant Fluhalp
tel +41 27 967 25 97
www.fluhalp-zermatt.ch

Täschalp Lodge and Restaurant
tel +41 27 967 23 01
www.taschalp.ch/lodge

Gandegghütte
tel +41 79 607 88 68

Hörnlihütte
tel +41 27 967 22 64
www.hoernlihuette.ch

Hotel du Trift
tel +41 79 408 70 20
www.zermatt.net/trift

Hotel Silvana
tel +41 27 966 28 00
www.hotelsilvana.ch

Monte Rosa Hütte
tel +41 27 967 21 15
www.monterosahuette.ch

Rothornhütte
tel +41 79 132 12 05

Schönbielhütte
tel +41 27 967 13 54

Täschhütte
tel +41 27 967 39 13
www.taeschhuette.ch

Ze Seewjinu (Ze Seewjinen)
tel +41 79 900 23 00
www.zeseewjinu.ch

Grächen, Randa and the Mattertal
Bordierhütte
tel +41 279 561 909
www.bordierhuette.ch

Saas-Fee and Saastal
Almagellerhütte
www.almagellerhuette.ch
tel +41 27 957 11 79

Berghotel Almagelleralp
www.almagelleralp.ch
tel +41 79 629 78 08

Britanniahütte
www.britannia.ch
tel +41 27 957 22 88

Mischabelhütte
www.mischabelhutte.ch
tel +41 27 957 13 17

Weissmieshütte
www.weissmieshuette.ch
tel +41 27 957 25 54

Camping in the Mattertal and Saastal

Zermatt
Camping Zermatt
Spissstrasse 17, 3920 Zermatt
(small tents only)
tel +41 79 536 46 30
email info@campingzermatt.ch
www.campingzermatt.ch

Täsch
Camping Alphubel
3929 Täsch
tel +42 27 967 36 35
email welcome@campingtaesch.ch
www.campingtaesch.ch
100 pitches

Randa
Camping Attermenzen
Kantonsstrasse, 3928 Randa
tel +41 27 967 25 55
email sommercamping@oberwallis.ch
www.camping-randa.ch

Saas-Grund and Unter den Bodmen

Camping Schönblick
3910 Saas-Grund
tel +41 27 957 22 67
email schoenblick@campingschweiz.ch
www.campingschweiz.ch

Camping am Kapellenweg
3910 Saas-Grund
tel +41 27 957 49 97
email camping@kapellenweg.ch
www.kapellenweg.ch

Camping Bergheimat
3910 Saas-Grund
tel +41 27 957 18 39

Appart- & Wellnesshotel Etoile
email apparthotel-etoile@bluewin.ch
www.top-of-saas.ch

APPENDIX B
4000m peaks

There are 36 separate summits over 4000m in the area covered by this guide.

Name	height (m)
Dufourspitze (Monta Rosa)	4634
Nordend (Monta Rosa)	4609
Zumsteinspitze (Monta Rosa)	4563
Signalkuppe (Monta Rosa)	4554
Dom	4545
Liskamm (Eastern summit)	4527
Weisshorn	4505
Täschhorn	4491
Liskamm (Western summit)	4479
Matterhorn	4478
Parrotspitze (Monta Rosa)	4432
Dent Blanche	4357
Ludwigshöhe (Monta Rosa)	4341
Nadelhorn	4327
Schwarzhorn	4322
Lenzspitze	4294
Strecknadelhorn	4241
Castor	4223

Name	height (m)
Zinalrothorn	4221
Hohberghorn	4219
Alphubel	4206
Rimpfischhorn	4199
Strahlhorn	4190
Dent d'Herens	4171
Breithorn (Western summit)	4164
Breithorn (Central summit)	4159
Bishorn	4153
Breithorn (Eastern summit)	4139
Breithorn (Gendarme)	4106
Pollox	4092
Breithorn (Roccia Nera)	4075
Ober Gabelhorn	4063
Dürrenhorn	4035
Allalinhorn	4027
Weissmies	4017
Lagginhorn	4010

APPENDIX C
English–German terms

English	German
accident	Unfall
accommodation	Unterkunft
saddle, pass	Sattel
alp	Alp
alpine club	Alpenverein
alpine flower	Alpenblume
avalanche	Lawine
B&B	Hotel garni
bakery	Bäckerei
bedrooms	Zimmer/ Schlafraum
bridge	Brücke
cable car	Drahtseilbahn, Seilbahn
cairn	Steinmann
campsite	Zeltplatz
castle	Schloss
chairlift	Sesselbahn
chamois	Gemse
chapel	Kapelle
church	Kirche
combe, small valley	Klumme
common room	Gaststube
crampons	Steigeisen
crest, ridge	Kamm
crevasse	Gletscherspalte

English	German
crevasse between glacier and rock wall	Bergschrund
dangerous	gefährlich
dormitory, simple accommodation	Matratzenlager, Massenlager, Touristenlager
east	Ost
easy	leicht
fog, low cloud, mist	Nebel
spring	Quelle
footpath	Fussweg/ Wanderweg
forest	Wald
glacier	Gletscher
gondola lift	Gondelbahn
gorge	Schlucht
greetings	Grüetzi
grocery	Lebensmittel
inn/guest house	Gasthaus or gasthof
hillwalker	Bergwanderer
holiday apartment	Ferienwohnung
hour(s)	Stunde(n)
ice axe	Pickel
information	Auskunft
lake, tarn	See

English	German
landscape	Landschaft
left (direction)	links
map	Karte
map sheet	Blatt
marmot	Murmeltier
moraine	Moräne
mountain	Berg
mountain guide	Bergführer
mountain hut	Alphütte
mountain inn	Berggasthaus
mountain path	Bergweg
mountaineer	Bergsteiger
roe deer	Reh
north	Nord
pass	Bergpass, Pass
pasture	Weide
path	Pfad
railway station	Bahnhof
ravine	Klamm
reservoir	Stausee
ridge	Grat
right (direction)	rechts
rock wall	Fels

English	German
rope	Seil
rucksack	Rucksack
scree	Geröllhalde
simple hotel	Pension
slope	Abhang
snow	Schnee
south	Süd
stonefall	Steinschlag
stream, river	Bach
summit, peak	Gipfel
torrent	Wildbach
tourist office	Verkehrsverein
upper	ober
vacancies	Zimmer frei
valley	Tal
via, or over	über
viewpoint	Aussichtspunkt
village	Dorf
water	Wasser
west	West
wooded ravine	Tobel
youth hostel	Jugendherberge

DOWNLOAD THE ROUTES
IN GPX FORMAT

All the routes in this guide are available for download from:

www.cicerone.co.uk/1075/GPX

as standard format GPX files. You should be able to load them into most online GPX systems and mobile devices, whether GPS or smartphone. You may need to convert the file into your preferred format using a conversion programme such as gpsvisualizer.com or one of the many other such websites and programmes.

When you follow this link, you will be asked for your email address and where you purchased the guidebook, and have the option to subscribe to the Cicerone e-newsletter.

www.cicerone.co.uk

NOTES

LISTING OF CICERONE GUIDES

BRITISH ISLES CHALLENGES, COLLECTIONS AND ACTIVITIES

Cycling Land's End to John o' Groats
Great Walks on the England Coast Path
The Big Rounds
The Book of the Bivvy
The Book of the Bothy
The Mountains of England & Wales:
  Vol 1 Wales
  Vol 2 England
The National Trails
Walking the End to End Trail

SHORT WALKS SERIES

Short Walks Hadrian's Wall
Short Walks in Arnside and Silverdale
Short Walks in Dumfries and Galloway
Short Walks in Nidderdale
Short Walks in the Lake District:
  Windermere Ambleside and Grasmere
Short Walks on the Malvern Hills
Short Walks in the Surrey Hills
Short Walks Winchester

SCOTLAND

Ben Nevis and Glen Coe
Cycle Touring in Northern Scotland
Cycling in the Hebrides
Great Mountain Days in Scotland
Mountain Biking in Southern and Central Scotland
Mountain Biking in West and North West Scotland
Not the West Highland Way Scotland
Scotland's Best Small Mountains
Scotland's Mountain Ridges
Scottish Wild Country Backpacking
Skye's Cuillin Ridge Traverse
The Borders Abbeys Way
The Great Glen Way
The Great Glen Way Map Booklet
The Hebridean Way
The Hebrides
The Isle of Mull
The Isle of Skye
The Skye Trail
The Southern Upland Way
The West Highland Way
The West Highland Way Map Booklet
Walking Ben Lawers, Rannoch and Atholl
Walking in the Cairngorms
Walking in the Pentland Hills
Walking in the Scottish Borders
Walking in the Southern Uplands

Walking in Torridon, Fisherfield, Fannichs and An Teallach
Walking Loch Lomond and the Trossachs
Walking on Arran
Walking on Harris and Lewis
Walking on Jura, Islay and Colonsay
Walking on Rum and the Small Isles
Walking on the Orkney and Shetland Isles
Walking on Uist and Barra
Walking the Cape Wrath Trail
Walking the Corbetts
  Vol 1 South of the Great Glen
  Vol 2 North of the Great Glen
Walking the Galloway Hills
Walking the Jura o' Groats Trail
Walking the Munros
  Vol 1 – Southern, Central and Western Highlands
  Vol 2 – Northern Highlands and the Cairngorms
Winter Climbs: Ben Nevis and Glen Coe

NORTHERN ENGLAND ROUTES

Cycling the Reivers Route
Cycling the Way of the Roses
Hadrian's Cycleway
Hadrian's Wall Path
Hadrian's Wall Path Map Booklet
The Coast to Coast Cycle Route
The Coast to Coast Walk
The Coast to Coast Walk Map Booklet
The Pennine Way
The Pennine Way Map Booklet
Walking the Dales Way
Walking the Dales Way Map Booklet

NORTH-EAST ENGLAND, YORKSHIRE DALES AND PENNINES

Cycling in the Yorkshire Dales
Great Mountain Days in the Pennines
Mountain Biking in the Yorkshire Dales
The Cleveland Way and the Yorkshire Wolds Way
The Cleveland Way Map Booklet
The North York Moors
The Reivers Way
Trail and Fell Running in the Yorkshire Dales
Walking in County Durham
Walking in Northumberland
Walking in the North Pennines
Walking in the Yorkshire Dales: North and East
Walking in the Yorkshire Dales: South and West

Walking St Cuthbert's Way
Walking St Oswald's Way and Northumberland Coast Path

NORTH-WEST ENGLAND AND THE ISLE OF MAN

Cycling the Pennine Bridleway
Isle of Man Coastal Path
The Lancashire Cycleway
The Lune Valley and Howgills
Walking in Cumbria's Eden Valley
Walking in Lancashire
Walking in the Forest of Bowland and Pendle
Walking on the Isle of Man
Walking on the West Pennine Moors
Walking the Ribble Way
Walks in Silverdale and Arnside

LAKE DISTRICT

Bikepacking in the Lake District
Cycling in the Lake District
Great Mountain Days in the Lake District
Joss Naylor's Lakes, Meres and Waters of the Lake District
Lake District Winter Climbs
Lake District:
  High Level and Fell Walks
Lake District:
  Low Level and Lake Walks
Mountain Biking in the Lake District
Outdoor Adventures with Children – Lake District
Scrambles in the Lake District – North
Scrambles in the Lake District – South
Trail and Fell Running in the Lake District
Walking The Cumbria Way
Walking the Lake District Fells –
  Borrowdale
  Buttermere
  Coniston
  Keswick
  Langdale
  Mardale and the Far East
  Patterdale
  Wasdale
Walking the Tour of the Lake District

DERBYSHIRE, PEAK DISTRICT AND MIDLANDS

Cycling in the Peak District
Dark Peak Walks
Scrambles in the Dark Peak
Walking in Derbyshire
Walking in the Peak District – White Peak East
Walking in the Peak District – White Peak West

SOUTHERN ENGLAND

20 Classic Sportive Rides in South East England
20 Classic Sportive Rides in South West England
Cycling in the Cotswolds
Mountain Biking on the North Downs
Mountain Biking on the South Downs
Suffolk Coast and Heath Walks
The Cotswold Way
The Cotswold Way Map Booklet
The Kennet and Avon Canal
The Lea Valley Walk
The North Downs Way
The North Downs Way Map Booklet
The Peddars Way and Norfolk Coast Path
The Pilgrims' Way
The Ridgeway National Trail
The Ridgeway National Trail Map Booklet
The South Downs Way
The South Downs Way Map Booklet
The Thames Path
The Thames Path Map Booklet
The Two Moors Way
The Two Moors Way Map Booklet
Walking Hampshire's Test Way
Walking in Cornwall
Walking in Essex
Walking in Kent
Walking in London
Walking in Norfolk
Walking in the Chilterns
Walking in the Cotswolds
Walking in the Isles of Scilly
Walking in the New Forest
Walking in the North Wessex Downs
Walking on Dartmoor
Walking on Guernsey
Walking on Jersey
Walking on the Isle of Wight
Walking the Dartmoor Way
Walking the Jurassic Coast
Walking the South West Coast Path
Walking the South West Coast Path Map Booklets
 – Vol 1: Minehead to St Ives
 – Vol 2: St Ives to Plymouth
 – Vol 3: Plymouth to Poole
Walks in the South Downs National Park

WALES AND WELSH BORDERS

Cycle Touring in Wales
Cycling Lon Las Cymru
Glyndwr's Way
Great Mountain Days in Snowdonia
Hillwalking in Shropshire
Mountain Walking in Snowdonia
Offa's Dyke Path
Offa's Dyke Path Map Booklet
Ridges of Snowdonia
Scrambles in Snowdonia
Snowdonia: 30 Low-level and Easy Walks – North
Snowdonia: 30 Low-level and Easy Walks – South
The Cambrian Way
The Pembrokeshire Coast Path
The Pembrokeshire Coast Path Map Booklet
The Snowdonia Way
The Wye Valley Walk
Walking in Carmarthenshire
Walking in Pembrokeshire
Walking in the Brecon Beacons
Walking in the Forest of Dean
Walking in the Wye Valley
Walking on Gower
Walking the Severn Way
Walking the Shropshire Way
Walking the Wales Coast Path

INTERNATIONAL CHALLENGES, COLLECTIONS AND ACTIVITIES

Europe's High Points
Walking the Via Francigena Pilgrim Route – Part 1

AFRICA

Kilimanjaro
Walking in the Drakensberg
Walks and Scrambles in the Moroccan Anti-Atlas

ALPS CROSS-BORDER ROUTES

100 Hut Walks in the Alps
Alpine Ski Mountaineering Vol 1 – Western Alps
The Karnischer Hohenweg
The Tour of the Bernina
Trail Running – Chamonix and the Mont Blanc region
Trekking Chamonix to Zermatt
Trekking in the Alps
Trekking in the Silvretta and Ratikon Alps
Trekking Munich to Venice
Trekking the Tour of Mont Blanc
Walking in the Alps

PYRENEES AND FRANCE/SPAIN CROSS-BORDER ROUTES

Shorter Treks in the Pyrenees
The GR11 Trail
The Pyrenean Haute Route
The Pyrenees
Walks and Climbs in the Pyrenees

AUSTRIA

Innsbruck Mountain Adventures
Trekking Austria's Adlerweg
Trekking in Austria's Hohe Tauern
Trekking in Austria's Zillertal Alps
Trekking in the Stubai Alps
Walking in Austria
Walking in the Salzkammergut: the Austrian Lake District

EASTERN EUROPE

The Danube Cycleway Vol 2
The Elbe Cycle Route
The High Tatras
The Mountains of Romania
Walking in Hungary

FRANCE, BELGIUM AND LUXEMBOURG

Camino de Santiago – Via Podiensis
Chamonix Mountain Adventures
Cycle Touring in France
Cycling London to Paris
Cycling the Canal de la Garonne
Cycling the Canal du Midi
Cycling the Route des Grandes Alpes
Mont Blanc Walks
Mountain Adventures in the Maurienne
Short Treks on Corsica
The GR5 Trail
The GR5 Trail – Benelux and Lorraine
The GR5 Trail – Vosges and Jura
The Grand Traverse of the Massif Central
The Moselle Cycle Route
The River Loire Cycle Route
The River Rhone Cycle Route
Trekking in the Vanoise
Trekking the Cathar Way
Trekking the GR10
Trekking the GR20 Corsica
Trekking the Robert Louis Stevenson Trail
Via Ferratas of the French Alps
Walking in Provence – East
Walking in Provence – West
Walking in the Ardennes
Walking in the Auvergne
Walking in the Brianconnais
Walking in the Dordogne
Walking in the Haute Savoie: North
Walking in the Haute Savoie: South
Walking on Corsica
Walking the Brittany Coast Path

GERMANY

Hiking and Cycling in the Black Forest
The Danube Cycleway Vol 1
The Rhine Cycle Route
The Westweg
Walking in the Bavarian Alps

For full information on all our
guides, books and eBooks,
visit our website:
www.cicerone.co.uk